Gonnae Gie's A Kick O' Yer Ba' Mister?

A tale of family and football by a fan
with a typewriter

ANTHONY HAGGERTY

FOREWORD

HUGH MACDONALD

The most powerful aspect of football is how it is replayed every day in our minds. We all have action replays we can call upon. They can include memories of those we have lost but who accompanied us to matches. The remembrances can encompass those moments when football invoked joy or prompted superficial despair that lessens over time like an old-inflicted bruise.

The sports journalist is given a prime view of much of this. Essentially, we are all fans with typewriters because football meant so much to us before we stepped into any press box. But we had to eschew much of this romanticism when reporting on the realities of the most powerful of professional sports.

One can, though, love the game, while encountering some of the uglier aspects of it. The memories of heroes shine down through the ages. The moment when brilliance dazzled us on dreich days can be recalled with ease. The names and scenes in the greatest of dramas never leave us.

Anthony Haggerty spent all of his working life casting an eye over football and reaching for his pen or bending over a keyboard. He has witnessed much and remains grateful to have done so. His insight is powerful but also wonderfully affectionate.

He has created his own memories, chosen his own heroes and been formed by a personal past. It is one that any football fan can recognise with regards to Anthony's passion and his deeply held affection. We have all been there in general terms.

His book, though, is a personal journey. It resonates with great names, it bounces with lovely anecdotes and observations, and it even contains a poem. It serves as a love letter to the beautiful game. It kicks off with King Kenny. It has, though, much to fascinate the commoner on the terracing or in the press box. It is a sporting life that is recogniseable to us all. So now over to Dalglish, Cooper, Best, Cruyff...and the day Tony met Diego.

ACKNOWLEDGEMENTS

I dedicate this book to:

My mother (Joan), my father (Daniel), my brother (Danny), my sister (Clare Frances), and my nephew (Matthew). I salute the best family unit in the world and for their unconditional and unwavering support and belief in me. You are behind me in everything that I do in my life and in particular this project. You are and always have been my inspiration for finally committing these thoughts and words to the pages.

Elizabeth Queen (My gran) who sadly passed away in February 1983 and whom I still miss dearly and love with all my heart to this very day.

Chris Roberts and Ronnie Mackay who were two terrific sports journalists and who are also no longer with us. Gone but not forgotten lads. I still miss my two friends big time.

Cliff Pike, my Hibs supporting friend who initially set me a Facebook challenge which just grew arms and legs. Cliff is a member of the Hibs TV crew and has a tremendous knowledge of football. I always enjoyed our chats at Easter Road fella. I'm glad you of all people finally got to see your beloved club win the Scottish Cup in 2016. Cheers Cliff and one final thing - GGTTH!

The Daily Record Sports desk for allowing me to use THAT iconic image on the front cover - Thank You very much. Cheers to photographer Dominic Cocozza for capturing the shot.

Everybody who encouraged me to take the plunge and stick this on Amazon. I was never that egotistical to think that anybody would read my book let alone pay for it! It's out there now guys, please buy it!

Diego Armando Maradona - RIP El D10S, enough said.

Caroline: Last but not least my darling wife Caroline. The definition of a true soulmate and the rock whom I cling to on a daily basis. Without you none of this would have been possible. You are my sounding board and best friend. I love you with every fibre of my being and I owe you everything.

CHAPTER 1

KING KENNY

It just had to be the King. King Kenny Dalglish. My first ever sporting hero was King Kenny. I was four going on five when I first clapped eyes on Kenneth Mathieson Dalglish.

I was taken to see Clyde as a kid because my father didn't want me tainted by sectarianism and bigotry from an early age. Craig Brown – who would go on to manage Scotland - was in charge of Clyde during the 1976/77 season. The 'Bully Wee' used to play at Shawfield Stadium which was in close proximity to Celtic Park in Glasgow.

My father and I had a ritual in the early days before his amateur team that he managed moved from the local Sunday pub league to bona-fide Saturday amateur league.

My dad would take me shopping to spend my weekly 'pocket money on Corgi cars. It was always Corgi cars.

Inevitably during the football I would run my cars up and down the wooden benches in the stand – there was plenty of room! Clyde didn't exactly pack them in.

One afternoon a roar went up, I knew what it was instantly. It was from Celtic Park and the supporters were letting rip at yet another goal for the Hoops.

I turned to my dad and said: "Do you think Kenny Dalglish has just scored for Celtic? Do you think Celtic are winning Dad?"

Needless to say we made the second half and I was in Paradise in more ways than one.

I had found my spiritual, football home. It was beautiful.

Going from watching Clyde to Celtic was like having a portable black and white TV set and then being able to afford a 50-inch colour TV.

It was life changing in more ways than one and let's face it Clyde were not Celtic.

My heart was racing... I was finally going to see Dalglish in the flesh. The King and I were going to be in the same place. For the rest of that season I watched on in awe as King Kenny helped guide Jock Stein's side to a League and Scottish Cup double.

It broke my wee brittle heart when he left Celtic for Liverpool for £440,000 in the summer of 1977. It was soul destroying. I thought I'd never feel the same way or ever love football again.

My dad tried to soften the blow by taking my brother and me to Anfield to watch King Kenny turning out for the Reds in 1978. I am not a Liverpool fan. I don't favour any English team in particular. You can only support one football team and anybody who tells you differently is not a true football fan.

I felt as if I couldn't support King Kenny at Liverpool with the same fervour and passion as I did when he played for Celtic. I'm eternally grateful though to my father for taking me along to see the King. The Anfield trip was great, don't get me wrong, it just wasn't the same. I never ever formed the bond or attachment with Liverpool or King Kenny that I probably should have.

During the game against Norwich, which Liverpool won 3-0, King Kenny didn't score and all I could think about was how Celtic were getting on. For the record, the Hoops were beating Partick Thistle 5-2.

I still loved King Kenny but in an entirely different way. Liverpool fans believed they would never replace Kevin Keegan when he departed for the Bundesliga in the summer of 1977 and signed for SV Hamburg. They were wrong and then some.

Within 12 months King Kenny had sumptuously lifted the ball over Bruges goalkeeper Birger Jensen at Wembley to score the winner in the 1978 European Cup Final after a glorious pass from fellow Scot Graeme Souness. I went mental of course but not as half as much as I would have done had Dalglish scaled the same heights with Celtic.

I have always followed King Kenny's career and his appeal never wanes. Although when you are a sports journalist you pretty much have to shed the hero-worship tag quickly.

Having said all that you can imagine my genuine surprise when I was sent along as the Daily Record's representative to be a guest of McDonald's and enjoy corporate hospitality at Hampden Park as Scotland entertained Germany during a Euro 2004 qualifier.

Kenny Dalglish was the host of the table. I mean King Kenny. Get in there. Food, drink, chit-chat with a genuine legend.

"There you go Tony, there's your ticket for the padded seats." "Cheers Kenny…or is it King?" I was feeling gallus by this point.

We make our way to the seats and then I hear the voice saying: "Tony, you're beside me."

I'm sitting alongside the legend that is King Kenny for a Scotland game at Hampden Park. I'm going to repeat that sentence because I didn't believe it myself at the time. I'm sitting alongside the legend that is Kenny Dalglish for a Scotland game at Hampden Park.

Kenny loves his country, he genuinely does. The national anthem was belted out with gusto. Fredi Bobic gave the Germans an early lead. Kenny kicked the seats in front, headed every ball, shouted and screamed passionately. We both told Scotland head coach Berti Vogts where he was going wrong.

I was in a state of football nirvana.

Then it happened. Kenny Miller equalised for the Scots with 20 minutes left to earn the team a deserved draw. Cue bedlam in the stands. King Kenny and I were going Tartan barmy in the corporate seats. I'm jumping around and pogoing with Dalglish as if he is my best mate.

I just closed my eyes and just had a moment as My mind drifted back to Shawfield during that early 1976/77 season. My formative years of being introduced to the beautiful game.

"Hey dad, where's my green Corgi Mini Cooper?"
"What's that roar Dad?"
"Do you think Kenny Dalglish has scored for Celtic?"
"Do you think Celtic are winning?"
"Hey dad, can you see me?"
"Hey dad I'm celebrating a Scotland goal with Kenny Dalglish…can you see me?"
"Hey dad, I wish you were here with me right now…as this is all down to you…"

I opened my eyes. This was as real as it got. I wasn't simply in the same place as greatness. I was genuinely up close and personal with Kenny Dalglish.

I didn't cry but I may as well have. I just wanted my dad to be with us both in that moment. I get emotional even thinking about it now.

Dalglish had his moments too as an interviewee whenever our paths crossed in a professional capacity. Let's just say he could be awkward and unhelpful at times…not all the time because on other occasions he could be charm personified. But that is by the by.

In my humble opinion, Liverpool got 10 times the player in King Kenny than they did with Kevin Keegan. Few players can hold a candle to Dalglish's ability as a footballer. He was a 10 out of 10 player – no argument. He is a football legend. An absolute icon.

King Kenny was my first football hero. He is the last world-class player in the truest sense of that statement that this country has ever produced.

Long live King Kenny.

King Kenny, Celtic, football and Corgi cars.

My whole blissful childhood summed up in seven words.

CHAPTER 2

SUPER TRAMP?

I loved John Robertson. He was a football genius. The man whom Brian Clough said this about,

"Give him a ball and a yard of grass, and he was an artist: the Picasso of our game."

That is high praise indeed. Clough was right though. Robertson was a gifted winger who produced when it mattered.

Check this out for a footballing C.V. if you don't believe me. Robertson scored the winning goal in a European Cup Final (1980 v Hamburg). He set up the winning goal in the European Cup Final (1979 v Malmo). He netted the winner in the League Cup Final (1978 v Liverpool). He coolly slotted the winner from the spot in an Auld Enemy clash at Wembley (1981). He scored for Scotland at the World Cup Finals (Spain 1982). He is a Scottish football legend.

Robertson achieved this despite suffering horrendous personal tragedies. Older brother Hughie and his wife Isobel died in 1979 after crashing the car he had given them. His daughter Jessica was then born with cerebral palsy and died at the age of just 13 in 1996.

Yet Robbo put the off-field problems behind him when he stepped on to a football field. He was the kind of player who got bums off seats. He drew comparisons to all the great wingers; Gento, Garrincha, Tom Finney, and Stanley Matthews. There was only one John Robertson.

He was Ryan Giggs long before the English Premier League appeared on the horizon. Nottingham Forest's European Cup-winning captain John McGovern expressed it best when he said: "John (Robertson) was like Giggs but with two good feet, not one. He had more ability than Giggs, his ratio of creating goals was better and over-all he was the superior footballer." Hell yeah, McGovern was right and then some.

When Clough's Nottingham Forest team bestrode Europe for two years, Robbo was the fulcrum of that team. Everything about them was beautiful, even the iconic red Adidas strip looked perfect. My father's amateur team wore the Forest replica kit back in the day. They never lost a cup final…go figure! Growing up I always equated that Forest strip with silverware and success, at professional as well as amateur level.

Clough really did have the whole world in his hands with his gang of rag-tag and bobtail players which he moulded into one of the best club sides English football has ever seen.

As for Robbo's value today, that would be in the multi-millions. He was a class act on and off the field. Robertson continued his success when he hung up his boots and became former team-mate Martin O'Neill's right-hand man with Wycombe, Norwich, Leicester, Celtic and Aston Villa.

I had the pleasure of interviewing Robbo back in 2015 to preview the magnificent Jonny Owen film 'I Believe in Miracles'. I also got to talk to Archie Gemmill and John McGovern, two of Robertson's fellow Scots in that wonderful Forest team.

Gemmill recounted a superb Clough anecdote. The midfielder had found out certain players were on more money than him and demanded a meeting with Clough. Gemmill rattled the manager's door then entered his office and screamed: "I'm not happy!" Before he could get another word in, Clough said: "Well which one are you Archie son?" There was a pause and an awkward silence. Gemmill revealed that it took nearly 15 minutes for him to realise that Clough was talking about The Seven Dwarves!

It was classic Clough.

The film was in honour of Clough's great side that brought the European Cup back to Nottingham in 1979 and 1980.

Robertson though turned out to be an absolute gem of a fella and I found him to be a humble, down to earth guy. He was absolutely brilliant with me.

An hour of his time was spent discussing Nottingham Forest, Clough, the film, Scotland, Celtic, his family tragedies. You name it, no topic was out of bounds. We both laughed and cried as we enjoyed a superb stroll down memory lane which was more like a limp down amnesia lane with the mind playing tricks on the two of us along the way. As a football journalist, such wonderful days reminiscing about the halcyon days are rare.

I really didn't want the phone call to end.

Robbo eventually hung up on yours truly by saying it had been an absolute pleasure. Let me reassure you John, the pleasure was indeed mine and for all those who got to see you play in the flesh. You are a legend and a gentleman to boot.

The definition of a true football winger. "We've got a wee fat guy who could run rings round any opponent and turn them inside out." Clough once said of Robbo. The legendary Forest boss also jokingly christened Robertson 'Super Tramp' because of his scruffy appearance and unkempt look. Robbo deliberately chose that title for his autobiography.

What a stellar career Robertson had. For any youngsters out there, I suggest you go and Google this guy. You won't regret it. I salute you, John Roberson and let's just say I do believe in miracles.

Super Tramp?

I'll never ever forget our chat John Robertson because it truly was wonderful, beautiful, magical.

CHAPTER 3

MOODY BLUE

Now this may come as a bit of a surprise to many who know where my footballing heart and allegiance lies. There was something about Davie Cooper that gripped me back then and still does now. I was a genuine fan of this guy.

Super Cooper scored one of the best goals I have ever seen. Sadly I never saw it live. It is still in my top three goals of all time. If you do not know the goal I am referring to then just look up the 1979 Drybrough Cup Final, where Rangers beat Celtic 3-1. Then sit back and marvel at Cooper's piece of football genius.

I don't care what team you support, this strike is a thing of beauty. Cooper's Hampden Park goal, with the grainy footage, has also taken on a mystical reverence since his untimely death from a brain haemorrhage in 1995.

No Rangers player since has given me that pit-of-the stomach feeling you got whenever the opposition's danger man picked up the ball because you knew something special was going to happen.

More often than not it did, especially when Cooper was around. I include the likes of Brian Laudrup and Paul Gascogne in that. Cooper was no less gifted than those two superb footballers.

Even the great Dutchman Ruud Gullit admitted that he was an admirer of Cooper. How's that for a compliment?

I cheered like a madman in 1985 the night Cooper kept his cool and scored the penalty against Wales that sent Scotland to the 1986 World Cup.

Cooper also played a starring role in one of the best Scottish Cup Finals in living memory. Motherwell's magnificent 4-3 triumph over Dundee United in 1991. Ask any Motherwell supporter of that era their take on Davie Cooper and they will wax lyrical for hours.

Rangers fans will tell you he was 'Simply The Best'. They are not far wrong. Davie Cooper's former Rangers manager Walter Smith summed it up best when he said: "God gave Davie Cooper a talent. He would not be disappointed with how it was used."

That largely explains why I stood in stunned silence and choked back tears at Glasgow Central Station when I stepped off the train to read the awful news in the Evening Times that Cooper had passed away in March 1995. It is still the only newspaper billboard that has stopped me in my tracks.

My best friend at Strathclyde University at the time was a guy called Martin Ogg. He adored Cooper. He was utterly distraught at the news. I felt compelled to do something, although I didn't know what to do or say to help him in his hour-and-a-half of need.

I was still a student at this time and we both used to attend creative writing classes. I grabbed a pen and paper when I got home and started writing.

Somehow these words just poured out on to the page I must apologise to Scots poet Tom Leonard – whom we were studying at the time – as well as Brian Clough and the indie band Sultans of Ping FC, whose words I may have borrowed for the purpose of the rhymes.

I typed them out on my word processor and sent the ode to Martin's hero through the post to his house in Falkirk. We then had a right good cry down the phone when the postman delivered.

I had to get an independent marker in to score the poem for my creative writing class. Let's just say I received one of the highest marks of my time at university which still makes me happy and very proud. The words get me all emotional, even today. It just reminds me of university and a golden era of watching football growing up.

I also dedicate this to two of my favourite Rangers-supporting pals, Ross Hunter and Cammy Murray, who also hero-worshipped Cooper. It was never really my intention to put this poem into the public domain and the pair of them have been trying to coax and cajole me into putting it out there for years. It's out there now fellas.

Most of all though I dedicate this to the one and only Super Cooper. Here is a humble homage and tribute. Signed an admirer who just happened to support the team from the other side of the city.

My 'Educated' Left Fit

Gie him a 'ba and a yerd o' grass.
He'd gie ye a move wi' a perfect pass.
Gie him a 'ba and a yerd o' space.
He'd gie you a move wi' godly grace.

Gie him a 'ba and a the sellik defence.
He'd beat five by playing keepie-up.
Gie him a 'ba and the sellik defence.
Cop yer whack fur the Drybrough Cup.

Gie him a 'ba and a set-piece kick.
He'd bend it, skelp it, swerve it - ken.
Gie him a 'ba and a set-piece kick.
Thank god fur nets as THAT free-kick ended up in the 'Glen...
(Rutherglen) that is.

Nicknamed Super Cooper.
We a' kent that it was true.
Bags o' skill and ability.
There wiz only wan 'Moody Blue'.

He cid put a ba' on a sixpence,
He cid hit shots like a bullet,
He wiz even adored and admired,
By the Dutch master Ruud Gullit.

Just gie him a 'ba and a full house crowd.
This entertainer wid send the Bears hame proud.
The man on the ba' who could dae anything.
"Davie, Oh Davie Cooper, Oh Davie Cooper on the wing."

In a Clydebank, Rangers, Motherwell and Scotland kit.
The No. 11 wi' the cultured left fit.

R.I.P.

CHAPTER 4

CHARLIE IS MY DARLING

From 1981 to 1983, when I was between the ages of nine and 11, Charlie Nicholas was my idol.

Nobody loved Champagne Charlie more than me

Actually, hold that thought – somebody did. It just happened to be my older brother Danny but more about him later.

Charlie was just brilliant. He exploded onto the Scottish scene and just couldn't stop scoring for Celtic. I adored him. I wanted to be him and when we played football outside in the streets, I was always Charlie Nicholas. He also had an uncanny knack of scoring against Rangers.

I can still hear the dulcet tones of Archie MacPherson commentating on two particular goals. A superb, swerving winner in a 2-1 victory at Ibrox in 1983: "He's aiming for goal himself, oh that's a brilliant goal!" Charlie celebrated with his trademark raised-knees dance in front of the Hoops faithful packed into the Broomloan Road Stand. The other was Charlie's debut goal for Scotland against Switzerland at Hampden that same year, when he flicked the ball from his right on to his left then volleyed home to cap a comeback from 2-0 down in a 2-2 draw. Cue Archie once again: "Here's Nicholas, He's done it, oh what a goal!"

It was wonderful stuff.

Charlie was uniquely & sublimely talented. A brilliant striker who had it all. The Cannonball Kid or Champagne Charlie. Either moniker suited him.

Charlie really did appear to have the world at his feet. He scored a beauty against Ajax in 1982 as Celtic somehow beat Johan Cruyff and Co over two legs in the European Cup. This guy could do no wrong in my eyes.

In November 1981, Charlie was even part of the Celtic team that won the Daily Express five-a-side tournament at Wembley Arena. He was tremendous as Celtic defeated the star-studded teams of Ipswich and Manchester United before turning over Southampton - who had Kevin Keegan in their team – in the final. The Celtic fans who tuned into Sportsnight were wowed by Charlie as no doubt the massive English audience were.

Just like Kenny Dalglish in 1977, my heart was smashed to pieces again when Charlie left to sign for Arsenal for £750,000 in the summer of 1983.

He bagged two penalties at Ibrox in his farewell appearance on an extraordinary day of action when Celtic, Dundee United and Aberdeen all stood a chance of winning the title on the last day of the season. Celtic rallied from two goals down at half-time to beat Rangers 4-2 that day. It wasn't enough as Dundee United beat city rivals Dundee 2-1 at Dens Park to claim their only Scottish Premier crown.

The Rangers fans did make me laugh that day as they taunted the Hoops supporters with a ditty to the tune of the 1970s hit 'Chirpy, Chirpy, Cheep, Cheep!' It went,
"Where's Yer Charlie Gone?
Where's Yer Charlie Gone?
Where's Yer Charlie Gone?
Far, Far, Away!"
Fair play to the Rangers fans as it was highly creative, even if the lyrics stung the Celtic fans to the core.
Charlie had Liverpool, Manchester United and Arsenal all chasing his signature but ended up choosing the Gunners. I always felt that he should have gone to Liverpool and played alongside his idol Dalglish. Perhaps then he would have fulfilled his destiny and won two of football's biggest prizes - the English title and the European Cup.

Fast forward a few years and I began working as a sports reporter for the Daily Record who just happened to have a Charles Nicholas Esq as their columnist.

We struck up a friendship that exists to this day. Charlie even had a nickname for me. He still refers to me as Kryptonite because of the Clark Kent glasses that I wore at the time. I did work for the Daily Planet...I mean Daily Record. How cool was it that Charlie had a nickname for me? I still laugh out loud whenever I think about it.

My hero-worship was something else. I even got the Charlie Nic end-perm hairdo monstrosity which he made famous during his Arsenal days. The haircut cost £50 which was a lot of money in the mid-1980s. It earned me a total ribbing in the school playground. I didn't care. I was gallus. I looked like Charlie Nicholas...or at least that's what I thought!

It drove my brother insane with jealousy. However, fate would help me repay everything to him. For as long as I remember, my brother always wanted to name one of his kids after Charlie Nicholas. I did say that nobody worshipped Charlie more than me except Danny. The trouble is that Danny had three girls. That didn't deter him. Girl No.3 duly arrived and I got the phone call to tell me the great news that I was an uncle again.

"I've named her Charlie Nichola after Charlie Nicholas…no 's' at the end…!"
"Are you serious, Dan?"
"Totally bro, I've already filled in the birth certificate!"

Danny was on his way to hospital to see his latest arrival for the first time. I congratulated him and hung up the phone. I then proceeded to dial Charlie and related the story that my brother had just named his daughter after him!

To Charlie's eternal credit and my brother's utter astonishment the next phone call he got was from his childhood hero. I explained that it would a mean the world to my brother to have Charlie Nic on the end of a phone. Charlie did exactly that. Danny was totally gobsmacked. The next phone call I received was from a tearful brother. It was one of the best feelings ever. We both got emotional down the phone.

As my brother later explained, Charlie Nic kicked it all off with the memorable opening line: "Is that Danny, it's Charlie Nicholas, have you just named your daughter after me? Can I just say one thing Danny, you are completely bonkers and your brother has a lot to answer for as I wouldn't do this for just anybody!"

You know that moment when your chosen occupation can be used as a force for everything that is good. Yeah, that!

It was a joyous and wonderful moment and the great thing about it is that I got to share it with my best pal who just happened to be my brother, the one I had shared so many football memories with growing up. Football journalism sometimes affords you some marvellous privileges at times. Danny worshipped Charlie Nicholas and I was totally made up for him.

Don't let anybody ever tell you that footballers don't care because they most certainly do. Charlie clearly cared. Footballers generally get a bad rap but some of them are wonderful human beings. I loved Charlie even more for taking time out to phone Danny, knowing what it would mean to him.

From 1981 to 1983 it's not really hard to understand why in football terms: 'Charlie was our darling'.

Nowadays we just worship a different Charlie altogether.
Take a bow Charlie Nichola.
P.S. I still love you too Charlie Nicholas.
Your friend always,
Kryptonite.

CHAPTER 5

THE NEW FIRM

Growing up in the 1980s we were introduced to a new concept in Scottish football - The New Firm. Sir Alex Ferguson and Jim McLean were two magnificent Scottish managers who moulded fantastic sides at Aberdeen and Dundee United respectively.

They were dubbed The New Firm by the media. For a wonderful period both Aberdeen and Dundee United challenged the duopoly of Celtic and Rangers at the top of Scottish football's pile. Both were also successful in Europe.

I hitched a magic carpet ride on Aberdeen's 1983 European Cup Winners' Cup run when they advanced all the way to the final and defeated the mighty Real Madrid on a memorable night in Gothenburg. I cursed Italian cheats Roma in 1984 as they swindled Dundee United out of a European Cup Final spot against Liverpool by nobbling the referee in the semi-final.

I also mourned the Tangerines' 1987 UEFA Cup Final loss to IFK Gothenburg after getting right behind them as they swept all before them. Dundee United thoroughly deserved a European trophy to show for their fantastic exploits in that era.

Willie Miller and David Narey were two players who epitomised both clubs during that time. Miller was a colossus for Aberdeen and a fantastic footballer. He arguably was the best penalty-box defender I have ever seen He was also one of the best tacklers and readers of a game ever.

Two images spring to mind when I think of Willie Miller. The iconic one-handed lift of the Cup Winners' Cup when the Dons became the Kings of Europe and there is his memorable celebration at Pittodrie after his headed equaliser against Celtic which gave the Reds the point they needed to clinch the 1984/85 Premier League title.

It is without a hint of exaggeration when I say that Miller could easily have slotted in beside the likes of Franco Baresi, Paolo Maldini or Claudio Gentile at the back. He was that good, the real deal.

Sir Alex Ferguson should have taken Miller to Manchester United when he departed for Old Trafford in 1986. Ferguson would have found the partnership he got with Gary Pallister and Steve Bruce a lot earlier if he had paired Miller with someone like Paul McGrath. Can you imagine that? It would certainly not have taken Ferguson four years to win his first major trophy if he had.

United stalwart Narey was as classy and elegant as any of the top-class players who have played in this country. He just oozed confidence. What Narey brought to the table was largely overlooked as he existed in an era of other superb players. Narey's talents possibly flew under the radar and he was probably not appreciated as much as he should have been.

Scotland boss Jock Stein knew his worth though and that's good enough for me. Narey's wonder strike against Brazil - the infamous 'toe-poke' as described by Jimmy Hill - at the 1982 World Cup gave me one of my most joyous moments in football growing up.

It was totally apt that Narey won the title with Dundee United in 1983 as they were a cracking side. Eleven years later I watched on in awe at Ibrox as a Narey-inspired Raith Rovers shocked Celtic in the 1994 League Cup Final.

The veteran's performance that day defied belief and he rightfully won the Man of the Match award. Like Miller, Narey could also have taken his talents to the biggest stages in England or Europe. He chose to shun the limelight though and I never ever got the chance to speak to him when I was a football journalist - more's the pity.

Cheers Dave, we'll always have Brazil 1982 and that infamous toe-poke!

Miller has since carved out a successful career as a pundit and he is just as much a class act off the pitch as he was on it. I was designated to phone Miller for the Daily Record when the devastating news of his former team-mate Neale Cooper's death broke in 2018. These are the calls that journalists dread but Miller could not have been any nicer. I had a couple of finger run-ups before I dialled the number.

Miller answered: "Hi Tony, let me compose myself." And off he went. He gave me 30 minutes of his time under circumstances that I could not really begin to imagine.

I never asked Miller a question, I didn't need to. I just let him speak. At the end of the call I said: "I'm so sorry Willie, I don't really know what to say to you." Miller replied: "Sometimes saying nothing works best, Tony. You respected the situation and I totally respect you for that. Thank you."

Miller was bang on, sometimes words are useless. It was a real touch of class from him taking the call in the first place. I never ever forgot that and I would like to think that Miller didn't either.

Maybe it's just me but I've always felt that for the years Aberdeen and United mounted a genuine challenge for honours, the sectarianism and bigotry associated with Celtic and Rangers abated. It was still there but nowhere near as prevalent as it is today. Both clubs had much more to worry them back then. The threat coming from the Granite City and Tayside was massive so the Old Firm had to channel their energy on Aberdeen and Dundee United rather than obsess about each other. That may be looking at Scottish football through rose-tinted glasses but I 'New Firmly' believe that.

The New Firm were a breath of fresh air. Aberdeen and Dundee United made Scottish football as competitive as it has ever been its illustrious history and everyone got right behind the two of them – especially in Europe.

For a while, there was much more to Scottish football than just Celtic and Rangers. It is wishful thinking to believe that those days may one day return to our game. They can't. They won't. Will they?

CHAPTER 6

THE BEST

My father was the manager of a highly successful amateur football team called Millerfield from 1977-1986. Opportunities to attend Celtic matches religiously were few and far between growing up but I vividly remember one occasion when my old man's side were not playing on a Saturday.

My dad took me to Easter Road to watch Hibs take on Celtic. "You might see something special. You'll thank me when you're older, son." Those were the exact words he used.

How there could be anything special about a player not bedecked in a Hooped jersey was beyond me. I was seven years of age back in January 1980. Yet I was to catch a glimpse of the fading talent that was George Best.

The Northern Irishman turned in a masterclass against title-chasing Celtic. Hibs were rampant and George was at his imperious best. He taunted Celtic all afternoon with clever passes, intricate play and darting bursts of speed here and there. The brain was still a willing participant even if the body wasn't quite in sync. Celtic were murdered 1-1.

The former Manchester United star was reputed to be on a whopping £1,500 a week when he turned up in Auld Reekie. It was obvious that the enigma was well past his best but the Northern Irishman could still pull the crowds as well as the birds.

Best was making his first competitive appearance against Celtic. He scored a cracker when he cut inside from the left and unleashed a beauty with his right foot that Hoops goalkeeper Peter Latchford saved. Unfortunately for Celtic, Latchford was three yards BEHIND the goal-line at the time, such was the ferocity of the shot which put Hibs 1-0 up.

Ally MacLeod smashed a penalty off the crossbar and Tony Higgins also hit the woodwork from two yards out before Roy Aitken scored an equaliser with a glancing header.

Best's talent had helped Hibs beat Rangers 2-1 on Boxing Day at Easter Road when he jokingly took a swig from a beer can that had been thrown at him by the opposition fans.

Despite being anchored at the foot of the table Hibs were chasing a rare Old Firm home league double. I was transfixed by Best in the famous Bukta Hibs kit. I even asked my dad to buy me a replica strip with Best and the No.11 on the back.

Who was this guy? He made football look easy. He was taking the piss out of the Celtic. "Hey dad, that's not right, nobody does that to the Celtic."

Best did.

As a student of the game, I was consumed by Best and began to research everything about him. I watched in awe and then marvelled at TV footage of his outrageous, impudent lob over Pat Jennings for Manchester United against Tottenham and his famous clenched-fist celebration. The sheer audacity of the dink, and the nonchalant execution by Best, are an absolute joy. It is vintage Best and one of my favourite goals.

I wasn't even born when Best scored that cracker in 1971. "Beautiful, absolutely beautiful", enthused Barry Davies in the Match of the Day commentary box. Quite. It is a fantastic goal and it always puts a big, stupid grin on my 'Chevy Chase' whenever I see it.

The greatest sportswriter who ever lived, Hugh McIlvanney, once said this of Eric Cantona: "He was no angel but he could play like the devil." The same rule applied to Best some two decades before the Frenchman's rise to fame.

BBC2 even dedicated a whole night of TV to George Best on his 50th birthday. It was a brilliant night of nostalgia and you almost felt not worthy of viewing such magnificence.

In football terms, a 'terrible beauty' was on display that day at Easter Road. This was Best in his latter-day pomp. It was mesmerising to watch. Big matches like the ones against Rangers and Celtic certainly flicked his switch and clearly got his juices flowing. That was the beauty. The terrible was the fact that we were witnessing a Best-before-end.

The glittering career was nearing its sell-by date despite a brief resurrection in the USA during the heady days of the NASL with the San Jose Earthquakes.

That didn't matter a jot to this seven-year-old. For one memorable Saturday, I saw the magic in all its beauty. Brazilian superstar Pele once remarked that Best was the greatest player he had ever seen. Just pause for a moment and take in those words. High praise doesn't even begin to cover that statement.

George Best is the finest footballer the United Kingdom has produced, bar none. I am proud to say that I witnessed the legend that was George Best once: "When I saw you, you looked like a diamond!"

The Belfast boy had filled my heart with pure joy and I totally loved the experience.

Incidentally, Celtic were pipped to the title in 1980 as Sir Alex Ferguson's Aberdeen claimed their first ever crown, with a 5-0 win over Hibs at Easter Road on the last day of the season. Hibs were relegated.

One final thing, although it may be 40 years too late.

I guess a 'Thank You Dad' is probably long overdue.

Cheers for that father.

You did good…in fact Dad, you're the Best.

CHAPTER 7

THE MAGNIFICENT 7

Chapter seven could really only be about the man they called the 'Magnificent 7'. I thought my days of hero-worshipping footballers were all behind me and over after Kenny Dalglish and Charlie Nicholas.

How wrong could I be?

I adored Henrik Larsson. The Super Swede. He is arguably the best piece of transfer business that Celtic have ever conducted, just £650,000 from Feyenoord. Wim Jansen knew exactly what he was doing when he brought Larsson to Scotland for the 1997/98 season which saw Celtic shatter Rangers' dreams of achieving the coveted 10-in-a-row.

I loved Larsson for the sheer unbridled joy he brought to me as a Celtic supporter and every other Hoops fan out there. Larsson just got it. He got what it meant to play for the club and the fans from the get-go. He became an integral part of the 'Celtic Family' instantly. Ask anybody of my generation and they will tell you that Larsson is the finest player they have seen in the Hoops. In my humble opinion, he is the best foreign player to have graced the Scottish game.

Larsson was class. When Martin O'Neill came to the club and teamed him up with Chris Sutton and John Hartson, he helped take Celtic to extraordinary heights.

I reported on two Old Firm games when I worked at the Daily Record. The 6-2 demolition derby in August 2000 when Larsson skinned Rangers defender Bert Konterman and chipped keeper Stefan Klos.

The goal is a thing of stunning beauty. Sky Sports commentator Ian Crocker rightfully stated that it was 'world class'. I was also at Ibrox for the final derby in that same 2000/01 season when Larsson notched his 50th goal of the campaign in typical fashion to seal a 3-0 victory. The Swede finished with 53 goals in a Treble-winning season and also scooped European football's Golden Boot.

Larsson's winning goal against Boavista in the UEFA cup semi-final in 2003, which helped put Celtic into their first European final for 33 years, also reduced my father and I to rubble. It is a moment etched in the hearts and minds of every Hoops fan.

Larsson also inadvertently allowed me to take my brother and father to the 2003 UEFA cup final in Seville.

Why?

I just happened to win £14,500 on the daily 49s lottery that's why!

I had gone to the bookies to put a bet on a Celtic victory but the odds were far too short. Instead I put a £2 stake on the daily lottery instead - 27, 7, 10, 2, 3 – it was the day, month and time that my first niece, Shannon Haggerty, was born. A meagre 7250/1 shot. The numbers came up earlier in the day and Larsson did the rest in the evening. That largely explained the tears as I sunk to my knees and told my dad we were all going to Seville because I could afford it.

Larsson didn't deserve to lose that night in Seville. He was super-human against Jose Mourinho's Porto and his two wonderful headers are testimony to that. There is also a horrible TV moment in the aftermath of the match when Larsson holds up his silver medal and turns to the camera, choking back tears as he says: "I didn't come here for this." It is s a poignant piece of footage and it hurts to watch it even now.

That's why nobody was more delighted for Larsson when he finally got his hands on a Champions League winner's medal when he came off the bench to help Barcelona beat Arsenal in the 2006 final.

Every Celtic supporter celebrated with Larsson that night as it truly felt we had all won the Champions League. After all Larsson was part of the Celtic Family. We had all won the cup with the big ears together.

Even Thierry Henry declared that night: "Arsenal never lost the final to Barcelona. We lost to Henrik Larsson". The duo would go on to become team-mates in the Nou Camp.

Do you know how many goals Larsson scored for Celtic? A whopping 242 in 315 games. The statistics are engrained in my mind.

I should know. I described every one of Larsson's goals at the behest of my Sports News editor Iain Scott for a tribute pull-out when Larsson left the club in 2004.

"Describe all 242 goals?"
"That'll take ages, boss."
"He'll love it Tony, trust me just do it, you know it makes sense..." was Scotty's reply.

One day in the office, legendary sports reporter Hugh Keevins was on the landline talking to ex-Rangers superstar Ally McCoist. His mobile phone rang. I picked it up. It was a foreign voice. I recognised it instantly and started shaking.

The Swedish superstar was on the other end of the line. I blurted out, well it was more of a shriek: "It's Henrik Larsson, it's Henrik Larsson...it's Henrik Larsson...!!!"
"Hi Henrik, it's Tony Haggerty, Hugh is on the other line, I'll just get him for you."

To which, in a Swedish accent that sounded akin to a Bond villain, Henrik said: "Aah, you described all of my goals when I left the club, my son Jordan loved it and kept it as a souvenir. Thank you for doing that."

It was enough. What more could you want? Hugh hung up on Ally and did his bit with Larsson. Ally, the great guy that he is, then phoned Hugh back and promptly hung up on him.

Hugh returned the call and Super Ally said: "Henrik Larsson, you hung the phone up on me to talk to Henrik f***ing Larsson! How many golden boots has he got?", (Larsson has one, McCoist has two!). It was a priceless comedic line from a brilliantly funny guy.

Many years later, I was at a function at Celtic Park and I knew Larsson was going to be there. He was sat beside Alan Stubbs at the table next to me. I had gotten to know Stubbsy really well during his time as manager of Hibs as I covered the Edinburgh beat for the Record.

I approached Stubbsy and asked him...well begged him really.. to introduce me to Larsson. This was my one and only chance. I was armed with a copy of the pull-out and a black marker pen. Stubbsy did as I asked and I am eternally grateful to him for that.

Initially Larsson looked at me and perused the pull-out, non-plussed. I then unmasked myself as the author. Larsson then hugged me, smiled and said: "Aah where do you want me to sign?"- "Anywhere is fine, Henrik" (or is it King of Kings?). Larsson replied: "In that case, I'll sign every page. It can be your own personal souvenir. Thank you again for doing this...it's great... yes I remember that hat-trick at Tynecastle very well...and good old Bert Konterman!"

Larsson was laughing. He then started reading out aloud some of my descriptions of his goals to Alan Stubbs as his eyes scanned the article.

True to his word he signed all the pages. It's hard to describe how I felt in that moment. It was another surreal yet wonderful episode in my career and life. Larsson duly put his moniker and the number 7 in black ink all over the pull-out.

Henrik was not a man of many words off the field as he much preferred to do all his talking on the park. My old boss Scotty was right about one thing though. Larsson did indeed love it. I owe Scotty a huge debt of gratitude for coming up with the original idea to describe all 242 Larsson goals. From the bottom of my heart Scotty, "Thank you boss." I now have a personal souvenir which will take some beating.

For seven wonderful years Larsson plied his trade in Scottish football. From 1997 to 2004, I totally idolised him. It was the kind of adulation I afforded Kenny Dalglish and Charlie Nicholas when I was growing up. I still worship Larsson to this day, a fabulously gifted footballer. Larsson truly was 'The Magnificent 7' and the 'King of Kings' at Celtic Park.

As they say in Sweden: "Tack for minnena Henke."

Thanks for the memories Henrik.

CHAPTER 8

FEVER PITCH

This is a bit left field. I never had any dealings with Dennis Bergkamp, I just totally admired the way he played football and went about his business.

The Premier League era ushered in all sorts of foreign imports but few were better than Bergkamp. He was of the finest players of his generation. Nicknamed the 'Non-flying Dutchman' because of his fear of flying, the former Ajax and Inter Milan star really came to prominence when he signed for Arsenal under Scotsman Bruce Rioch for a bargain £7.1million in 1995.

Bergkamp had grace, poise, guile and an almost balletic quality. He never sprinted or ran, he just seemed to glide across a football pitch. He rejuvenated the Gunners under Arsène Wenger as well as his own career. He helped them win three Premier League titles and four FA Cups. The Gunners also reached the 2006 UEFA Champions League Final, which they lost 2-1 to Barcelona as the Dutchman watched on from the bench in his last act before retirement.

Bergkamp possessed one of the most natural techniques of any Dutch international and that is saying something considering there has been a few wonderful technicians from the Netherlands. Former team-mate Thierry Henry rated him 'a dream for a striker'. Bergkamp also finished third twice in the FIFA World Player of the Year award and was selected by Pelé as one of the 100 greatest living players.

There are many Bergkamp career highlights, such as his magnificent hat-trick against Leicester City at Filbert Street or his quite stunning last-minute winner against Argentina at the 1998 World Cup in France.

There could only be one winner in my mind and that was his astonishing goal against Newcastle. It was world class and quite rightly voted the best Premier League goal 25 years after the competition's inception. It will probably still be voted the best Premier League goal after 50 and 100 years. I have never seen a goal like it before or since.

It is a piece of absolute genius, brilliantly crafted by a Dutch master at work. The technique, balance, poise, control, composure, coolness, clinical finish - it's all there in this mesmerising piece of skill. It's not skill actually, it's art. Everything about it is beautiful.

The late and very great BBC commentator Kenneth Wolstenholme famously described Brazil's fourth goal by Carlos Alberto in the 1970 World Cup Final thus: 'Oh, that's sheer delightful football!'

This is another piece of sheer delightful football. It is why we fall in love with the game, the moments that take your breath away. Bergkamp was that kind of player who could make you fall in love with football over and over again. In a league awash with cash you got the impression that Bergkamp didn't care about any of that. He was here simply to entertain us and show every supporter the true meaning of the 'beautiful game'. It was inevitable that glory and honours would follow.

It says everything that Bergkamp's own heroes growing up were Johan Cruyff and Glenn Hoddle as he certainly modelled his own game on them. He somehow managed to fuse the two and create a hybrid.

Did you know that Bergkamp was named after Scots football legend Denis Law? I did speak to Denis Law once or twice when I was at the Daily Record and he was a wonderfully kind and generous man who defined the word 'legend'. I remember once phoning the Lawman to ask if he was supporting England at the World Cup Finals in 2002.

Law said: "Will I be supporting England? Why would I do that? I'm Scottish!" I burst out laughing. For the one and only time in my career, I let my professionalism slip and I replied: "Denis Law, I love you." He replied: "I love hearing a broad Scottish accent, you're not so bad yourself kid! Phone me anytime you want Tony and I'll endeavour to be of assistance." How classy is that?

It carried as much class as the clip of his namesake skinning Newcastle defender Nikos Dabizas that fateful day at St James' Park. Just take a moment to truly dissect the utter beauty of Bergkamp's goal. I could watch it on repeat for the rest of time. It never fails to make my heart skip a beat.

I never did get to see Denis Law in the flesh. He was before my time. Although I did see Dennis Bergkamp though as I specifically made the trip to Ibrox to take in a pre-season friendly in 2003 just to watch the great Dutchman. Arsenal ran out easy 3-0 winners but I never ever got the opportunity to speak to him.

Why did I latch on to Bergkamp? Of all the foreigners to play in the English game, he just stood out. Bergkamp truly played football the way we all want to see it. He made the game look easy, the most difficult skills look so simple. He did it all as if it was the most natural thing in the world. It was like every time he took to the field he was enjoying a kickabout in the park with his mates. Bergkamp played football and entertained like it was the law…man!

Whenever or wherever Bergkamp displayed his sublime talents for Arsenal he often got me into a state of 'Fever Pitch'.

How apt is that?

CHAPTER 9

JOE-HAN 'NOSE' THE SCORE

One of the great things about growing up in the 1980s was going along to Celtic Park for midweek European games.

For a three-year spell, Celtic played host to European football royalty, pitting their wits against the heavyweights of Real Madrid, Juventus and Ajax.

Long before the Champions League came into being, the competition was called the European Cup.

It was a wonderful tournament but in 1992/93 it was sabotaged by greedy, corporate Gordon Gekko business types. These men sacrificed the greatest club competition on earth at the altar of cash and all for their own ends.

Gone were the round-robin days when you drew a team and took your chance over two legs. The suits couldn't bear the likes of Real Madrid, Juventus or Ajax crashing out at the early stages so they contrived this aberration – the Champions League – which is as far removed from the spirit of the original tournament as you can possibly imagine.

The new rules ensured that clubs such as Celtic, Steaua Bucharest, Red Star Belgrade, Aston Villa, Nottingham Forest, Feyenoord and PSV Eindhoven would never get their hands on the big trophy again. It was the death knell for European football's Cinderella stories.

But in the 1980s, Celtic took on the best of the best in the European Cup. I can remember vividly when Johan Cruyff and Co came to Glasgow. My father had always encouraged me to watch the opposition whenever somebody good visited.

Ajax weren't just a good side, they were great. They seemed to be on the verge of something special again, almost a decade on from when Cruyff led them to three successive European Cup triumphs from 1971-1973.

"Ooft, it's a tall order tonight son but do yourself a favour and watch Johan Cruyff."
"You'll like him."
"Who?"
"Joe Han whit?"

Needless to say, what followed at Celtic Park served as another football education. This 'Joe Han Cryff' geezer turned out to be amazing although Celtic played out of their skins to earn a 2-2 draw.

"This Joe Han guy is the business da' is he no?"
"What a plerr he is man...we're gonna get cuffed in the second leg, aren't we?"

Cruyff was nearing the twilight of his career when he pitched up at Celtic Park. He had returned to his first love after revolutionising Barcelona then finished his playing days with a stint at Ajax's deadly rivals Feyenoord, whom he miraculously guided to the Dutch title.

Barcelona under Pep Guardiola would never have existed had it not been for Cruyff, who returned as manager to usher in an even greater era of success at the Nou Camp. You can't even begin to fathom the way this guy perceived football.

Cruyff was 'Total Football'. He ate, slept and drank the game. Some of his musings on the concepts of space and time in football are absolutely mind blowing.

Cruyff thought about football on a spiritual, intellectual, and philosophical plain that seemed beyond our grasp and comprehension.

It wasn't really. It was all common sense and very simple. Football wasn't just sport to Cruyff. It was an art form and it was also a religion he practiced daily. It was a way of life for him.

Two of my favourite football books are 'Ajax, Barcelona, Cruyff' and his autobiography 'My Turn'. If you ever have the opportunity then please read both of these books and you'll see exactly what I mean.

Cruyff was a snooker player on a football field. He was three moves ahead of everybody else at all times. It was extraordinary to see at close quarters. He just knew where to be and where the ball was going three passes before it reached its destination.

Total football. Totally captivating. It had me in raptures.

I had to study this guy Cruyff in more depth. I duly did my homework. He took my breath away at Celtic Park that night, he really did. Watch the footage, you will not be disappointed.

Ironically Cruyff gave away a penalty at Celtic Park after falling for a bit of trickery by Tommy Burns. Fair enough, he was slowing up in his old age but what happened next was utterly magnificent.

Not long after Cruyff raced up the other end and hit a sublime, cushioned volleyed through ball from Jesper Olsen's wayward pass and parted the Celtic defence like the Red Sea. Soren Lerby's dink over Pat Bonner is sensational too but it would not have been possible had it not been for Cruyff. There he was in his late 30s, directing traffic against Celtic and just being, well...Cruyff to be honest.

My abiding memory of that game is that Cruyff pass. It is just magical. It is also another goal and piece of sublime skill that I could watch on a loop. I love everything about it.

Anthony Haggerty

I can even hear the late, great STV commentator Arthur Montford in my head. The bold Arthur would probably have summed it all up succinctly thus: "Olsen, Cruyff, Lerby goal...sensation Ajax back in front!" Super stuff.

The Holy Trinity of football has always been Pele, Maradona, Cruyff. He remains a Dutch master and the finest player the Netherlands has ever produced.

What will have pleased Cruyff most about football is the fact he has entered the lexicon of the game – 'The Cruyff Turn.' Imagine being so utterly gifted as a footballer that they named a piece of skill after you. Of all the football greats, nobody else has a move named after them, do they? Not to my knowledge.

Cruyff saw football in pictures. 'The Cruyff Turn' was not the work of a footballer but an artist. The football pitch was Cruyff's blank canvas and he was a most wonderful painter.

That is why I feared the worst for Celtic in the return leg in the Olympic Stadium in Amsterdam. I remember tuning into Radio Clyde and Richard Park or Jimmy Sanderson uttering the immortal line: "It looks like Graeme Sinclair is going to do the marking job on Cruyff!"

I switched the radio off laughing. It was a nervous laugh. "What is Big Billy thinking? How can a guy that cost £65,000 from Dumbarton days before mark Cruyff? I know Cruyff plays for Ajax but he will literally take Sinclair to the cleaners!"

Amazingly, he didn't.

The European Cup threw up one of those good old-fashioned football shockers as Sinclair had the game of his life and put the shackles on Cruyff. Courtesy of a fantastic goal from Charlie Nicholas and a last-minute counter from George McCluskey, Celtic miraculously won 2-1 in Holland. It was an astonishing feat and a stunning result. David had toppled Goliath.

A decade later, I watched on TV as Cruyff led Barcelona to their first European Cup triumph at Wembley in 1992. Ronald Koeman's wonderful free-kick strike edged out Gianluca Vialli and Roberto Mancini's swashbuckling Sampdoria in a cracking end-to-end final.

I cheered madly at the final whistle in a student house full of Italians. They screamed obscenities, hurled all sorts of insults at me and told me to vacate the premises. It was an offer I couldn't understand, never mind refuse.

The modern day Barca owe everything to Cruyff. The day Cruyff died I was crestfallen. I don't know why I was so devastated as I'd never met him and our paths had never crossed. The Record decided to do another one of those pull-outs in tribute to him. Only the great and the good get a pull-out. Cruyff was both.

I came up with the bright idea of getting hold of Graeme Sinclair. Little did I know it would give me one of the most satisfying and pleasurable moments of my journalistic career.

I duly spoke to Sinclair and he gave me one of the greatest lines ever. I asked him to talk me through that night against Ajax and how he did the man-marking job on Cruyff. Sinclair said: "Johan Cruyff was one of the greatest players to have ever played the game. He is a football legend and a global icon. Yet whenever my wife sees Cruyff she refers to him as the guy that broke my nose and caused me to have a snoring problem!" You could not make it up. It was a wonderful story and manna from heaven for a tabloid journalist.

Sinclair explained how Celtic manager Billy McNeill initially wanted him to shackle Jesper Olsen who ran riot in the first leg. However, big Billy had a last-minute change of heart and Sinclair was detailed to stifle Cruyff. Sinclair said: "I got the instructions, if Cruyff goes to the toilet, you go with him!"

It turns out Cruyff had accidentally banjoed Sinclair with a flailing arm and broke his nose. Smelling salts and two bits of cotton wool rammed up the nostrils of Sinclair's hooter sufficed as a patch-up job, above his blood-stained jersey. At one stage near the end, Cruyff just threw his hands up in the air exasperated as the Celtic midfielder carried out McNeill's word to the letter.

The rest is history.

I conjectured that maybe Cruyff had broken Sinclair's nose because he had decided it was 'His Turn'...to get it. We both laughed out loud at that. In the darkness of Cruyff's death there was at least some light and dark humour. It was a small crumb of comfort but I took some solace in it.

Sinclair may well have had the last laugh on Cruyff in that particular joust. It was a rare occasion when Cruyff was a loser. Football was the biggest loser the day this great man passed away. Sometimes the beautiful game can turn downright ugly.

If I ever go to heaven and it turns out that there are football pitches in the sky, then I know whose team I want to be in. And when it becomes 'My Turn' to pick players for my side then I choose Johan Cruyff...every single day of the week.

For the time being, rest in peace 'Joe Han'.

CHAPTER 10

PERFECT 10, IMPERFECT PICTURE

What follows is a party-political broadcast on behalf of the FoDAM party (Friends of Diego Armando Maradona) in homage to the greatest player of all time.

When Maradona came along my football world spun on its axis. Even his name tripped off the tongue, it seemed exotic and wonderful, almost other worldly.

My love affair with Diego began in 1979. I had heard all about this wonder kid even before I had watched him kick a ball. Luis Cesar Menotti deemed him not good enough to play for Argentina when the host nation won the 1978 World Cup.

Maradona was already making waves for Boca Juniors at club level. The least said about Scotland's World Cup efforts in 1978 the better. Maradona didn't feature in that tournament but as luck would have it the following summer Argentina came to Scotland to play at Hampden.

It was June 1979, and I was six years old. My dad got tickets and took me and my older brother Danny along to Hampden, telling us to watch Maradona. As if I was ever going to do anything else. I was transfixed.

There is a famous clip of Maradona warming up to the Opus III song 'Live Is Life' during his pomp at Napoli. He is keeping the ball up in time to the music. Yet Maradona was doing this same routine at Hampden back in 1979. He could hit the crossbar at will with a ball from 20-30 yards long before the crossbar challenge was invented. He could play keepie-up with anything. Tennis ball, golf ball, squash ball, water bottle, you name it. I swear if you'd thrown a set of bagpipes at Maradona that day then he would have juggled them with both feet and kept them in the air too!

Maradona's party piece that day was something to behold. He fired a football high up into the air and then on the drop floated the most audacious chip from almost 80 yards which travelled the length of the Hampden field and bounced right in front of the marching pipe band.

The SFA believed a pipe band belting out tunes such as 'Amazing Grace' passed as entertainment at Scotland internationals. It was the 1970s after all! Maradona was amazing when the match started as well, tearing the Scots to pieces. He also netted his first international goal, tricking Scotland keeper George Woods with a dummy before planting a cracking shot in at his near post. It was a brilliant piece of skill in a virtuoso display that saw Argentina run out 3-1 winners.

A star was born.

I had never seen anything like Maradona. Fast forward three years and I cried tears of disappointment when the 1982 World Cup ended in disaster for my new international sporting hero. Maradona was sent off in disgrace against Brazil for losing the rag. He had an absolute nightmare against Argentina's bitter rivals.

That came just days after a brutal clash against the Italians and a match-up with notorious Juventus defender Claudio Gentile that has gone down in football folklore. When people talk about the greatest of all-time my answer is always the same - Maradona. It's not Pele, Johan Cruyff, Lionel Messi or Cristiano Ronaldo. It is Maradona and I will endeavour to tell you why.

If the comparison for great players is how would they have coped in another's era then I would urge everybody to dig out a recording of Italy v Argentina in the 1982 World Cup. Watch the full 90 minutes. Maradona was fouled by Gentile a staggering 23 times.

It is a world record for the most fouls on any one player in any one game. Think about that statistic - it equates to a foul by Gentile on Maradona almost every four minutes. It is a statistic that fascinates and intrigues me to this day. It is incredible and unprecedented. It simply would not be allowed in the modern-day game.

We are not talking niggly fouls here, we are talking leg-breakers, crunchers, knee-high jobs, career-enders, the lot. Maradona faced that kind of treatment in almost every 90 minutes he played. It didn't matter if he was turning out for Boca Juniors, Barcelona, Napoli or Argentina. Players did not want simply to foul him. They wanted to maim him or end his career.

The butcher of Bilbao – Andoni Goikoetxea – almost succeeded. When you see Goikoetxea's horrific tackle on Maradona in slow motion it defines the footballing term 'shocker'. It is a brutal challenge which shattered and snapped Maradona's ankle ligaments. It even threatened to finish his playing days back in 1983 when he played for Barcelona.

So the next time people bang on about Messi or Ronaldo being the best player ever, show them a re-run of Goikoetxea's challenge as well as the Italy v Argentina clash at the 1982 World Cup and pose a simple question.

Could Maradona in his prime have played in today's game? The answer is a resounding yes. Could Messi or Ronaldo have played back then? I do not think so.

Both players are protected species and the dark arts of defending have long since been outlawed. Gentile would be banned sine-die if he were playing the game today.

It is all conjecture and speculation of course. Nobody has come up with a more convincing argument yet - at least to me - as to why any player other than Maradona should be lauded and voted as the best ever.

Diego recovered from that brutality and returned to World Cup action in 1986. Maradona and Argentina were looking every inch the winners from early on in Mexico. The mood of the tournament changed for their last-eight tie with England as politics and sport began to mix. The lines became fuzzy because we were set for a re-enactment of the Falklands War.

Argentina had invaded the Falklands in 1982 and laid claim to the disputed British territory they called Las Malvinas. Under Prime Minister Margaret Thatcher, Britain declared war and after 10 weeks Argentina finally surrendered, suffering heavy losses as the islands remained in British hands. The quarter-final during Mexico '86 was the first time the nations had faced each other on a football field since the war.

The lead-up to the clash was ugly to say the least. There was a bitter football history too after World Cup winning boss Sir Alf Ramsey had branded Argentina 'animals' for the way they had played in the 1966 quarter-final. Argentina's captain Antonio Rattin was sent off in the match but refused to leave the field and was finally escorted off the hallowed Wembley turf by the police as it all threatened to get out of hand.

It is fair to say revenge was very much on Argentinian minds in this match. As a Scotsman and Maradona fanatic, I am not ashamed to say I was supporting Argentina. That is just how it was.

What happened in the match still causes many an Englishman to twitch as Argentina won 2-1. Maradona scored the two most famous goals ever seen at a World Cup. The first was a handball and let's not beat about the bush here – the little genius cheated. As Maradona said himself: "I acted like a thief, I picked the English pockets." Calling it the 'Hand of God' goal only served to add insult to England's injury.

The second goal is not up for question. If football can be expressed as a work of art then this is it splashed all over the canvas. Think Leonardo Da Vinci's 'Mona Lisa' or Edvard Munch's 'The Scream'. It is a masterpiece. If there is a definition of poetry-in-motion then this is it. Watching Maradona slaloming his way past player after player like an Olympic skier before sliding the perfect finish past Peter Shilton is a joyous moment in sport.

It remains the greatest goal of all time. Name a better one? It wasn't voted the 'Goal of the Century' for nothing. It will never be beaten.

El Diego had done a number on the Auld Enemy. He was an honorary Scotsman. He was my Diego. I loved him unconditionally by then.

Every time I see Maradona, I picture both of those goals against England in my head. Ridiculous to the sublime.

I have three favourite Maradona goals. The other is an exquisite free-kick which he dispatched with ease against Juventus. It proved to be the winner in a significant 1-0 Serie A win for Napoli at the San Paolo in 1985. It was also an indication that the balance of power in Italian top-flight football was shifting towards Naples. Napoli and Maradona would win their first Scudetto in 1986/87 and repeat the feat in 1989/90.

They call Diego Armando Maradona 'Dios' (God) in both his home country and Naples. He led the unfashionable Neapolitans to their golden era, winning the Scudetto twice, the UEFA Cup, the Super Cup and the Coppa Italia.

It is the equivalent of taking a team like Partick Thistle to the very top of Scottish and European football.

They have just released a documentary film, called 'Diego Maradona' that charts his time in Napoli. It should be part of every high school or university curriculum. Saying it is brilliant is doing the word a total disservice. It is compulsive viewing and a must-watch for football and non-football fans alike.

I never thought I would ever get to see Maradona in the flesh again but in 2008 something inexplicable happened. Argentina visited Scotland again and it just happened to be Maradona's first outing as national team manager.

By now I was a sports journalist for the Daily Record, I couldn't get to meet my football idol – could I? No way - dream on. Miraculously that dream became a reality.

I was given a glass trophy with a hand cupping a ball and the inscription: 'To Maradona, on behalf of the people of Scotland, for scoring the 'Hand of God' goal against England in 1986. Thank You!'

Argentina were training at Celtic Park on the night before the match. I was despatched to Paradise with the simple instruction take the trophy and get a picture of El Diego, Dios, Diego Armando Maradona, holding it. No chance. You couldn't get near him. Security was frightening.

The only time Maradona was alone was when he was out on the Celtic Park turf, instructing his team. I positioned myself at the mouth of the tunnel. The session ended and the legend made his way towards the dressing room. It was now or never.

"Diego, Diego, Diego, a gift from the people of Scotland!" I screamed at him. He walked by but all of sudden he turned back. I held out my hand, bearing the glass trophy.

He ambled towards me. "For me?" "Yes Diego, it is for you from the people of Escocia for dos goals against Angleterre." I spat that sentence out, trying my best to communicate in broken Spanish. Maradona allegedly doesn't speak any English. He just nodded and laughed. Maradona took my trophy...he took the trophy from my grasp. "Gracias senor."

I was sliding down the wall of the tunnel at this point and a steward came hurtling towards me to disrupt proceedings. He was met with a flying kick to the 'Denis Laws' as my photographer Dominic Cocozza appeared from nowhere. He flashed his camera lightning quick as I strained every sinew to stretch my arm around a football icon. It was pandemonium as all hell broke loose. Police, security staff and stewards all started to wade in.

I did not care. I had a back-page story and a photograph of sorts of Maradona holding the glass trophy, courtesy of Dominic.

My brother has never really forgiven me for having my picture featured on the back page alongside Maradona. I'm really sorry Danny…it's a dirty job at times but somebody has to do it! Somebody pinch me, did this really happen? Some weeks later a random guy in a club in East Kilbride approached me and asked to shake the hand that shook the 'Hand of God'!

The real beauty though lies in the fact that it is a totally imperfect picture of the perfect No.10.

Every football fan has their own memories of Maradona, a favourite goal or story. For a spell in the 1980s, Maradona was the most famous footballer in the world.

Everybody has their own thoughts on Diego - the highs, the lows, the drugs. I've always struggled with the concept that the drugs Maradona took during his playing career were performance enhancing. Life threatening? Yes. Performance enhancing? Most certainly not. Maradona and performance enhancing drugs? Really? The sentence is an oxymoron. As if Maradona would have needed any stimulants to enhance his performance. Like Muhammad Ali in the ring, Maradona was the greatest bar none on a football field.

I prefer to remember the Maradona who scored the goal of the century against England at the Mexico World Cup in 1986.

Argentine commentator Victor Hugo Morales nailed it completely when he famously uttered these words in the commentary box during that match:

"There goes Maradona.

"Two men on him…

"He goes on the right side.

"The genius of world football.

"He can pass it to Burruchaga…always Maradona.

"Genius…Genius…Genuis…ta…ta…ta…ta…Gooooal…Goooooal …I want to CRYYYY…Holy God…long live Football!!!"

"Gooooalzilla…Diegoal…Maradona…this makes me crrryyy…I'm sorry…Maradona on an unforgettable run…in the best play of all time…COSMIC KITE!!!"

"What planet did you come from…to leave all the English in your wake…to make a whole nation scream as one?

"Argentina…2 England…0…Diegoal! Diegoal!

"Diego Armando Maradona…Thank You God…Thank you for football…for Maradona…for these tears. This is Argentina…2 England…0!"

Indeed Hugo…indeed! I don't think as a sports journalist I could have expressed a goal of that magnitude any better myself.

To the diminutive powerhouse who scored those two unforgettable goals in the 1986 World Cup against the Auld Enemy. The No.10 who conquered the world and achieved his destiny and dream of holding that famous gold trophy in his hand.

Thank You God, Thank You for football, Thank you for Diego Armando Maradona.

Diego Armando Maradona. You had me enchanted from six years of age and 42 years later my love for you burns as brightly and as passionately as ever.

RIP El D10S.

'Gracias senor' for everything.

CHAPTER 11

THAT'S-A-NO-FOOTBALL
THAT'S-A-GARBAGE!

Ruud Gullit rose to prominence in 1987 when he moved from PSV Eindhoven to AC Milan for a then world record transfer fee of £6million.

He was part of a Dutch trio that upped sticks for the San Siro along with Marco Van Basten and Frank Rijkaard. Gullit helped the Italians to three Serie A titles and two successive European Cups. He also captained Holland to European Championship glory in Germany in 1988.

In 1996 he signed for Chelsea as player-manager and in his debut season led the Blues to FA Cup success. It was the club's first trophy for 26 years and he became the first overseas manager to win the FA Cup. Gullit also won the Ballon d'Or in 1987. He was a true baller.

So how did this Dutch master end up at Almondvale in Livingston, fending off questions from me and my dad?

My father was a salesman to trade. His van delivered pies, sausages, black pudding, haggis, pizzas to chip shops in and around the Glasgow area. Always self-deprecatory, he would describe himself as a 'minky pieman'.

The chip-shop trade in Glasgow is full of Italians. My father just happened to befriend an Italian fryer named Sandro who worked in one of the shops on my old man's run. Sandro was a mad AC Milan supporter. He also had a soft spot for Celtic too having lived in Scotland for many years but loved the Rossoneri with all his heart.

When Gullit, Van Basten and Rijkaard were in their pomp at the San Siro, Sandro was in his element. When AC Milan won back-to-back European titles, Sandro invited my father and I up to his club in Muirhead where he would regularly watch his heroes on an Italian satellite channel.

During the discussions between Sandro and my dad in the shop, the Italian had convinced himself that he needed a more regular football fix. He bought a season ticket for Parkhead for the 1988-89 season. That proved to be a terrible move as Celtic were commencing a slump that would see Rangers win the next nine league titles. Undeterred, Sandro would watch the Hoops on a Saturday then tune in to watch his beloved AC Milan at the club on a Sunday. He was a well-known face and a raconteur in the privacy of his club. Like most Italians, Sandro was demonstrative…very demonstrative. The clash in football contrasts could not have been starker. Celtic were rank rotten. AC Milan were rampant.

Whilst Sandro was watching Gullit, Van Basten and Rijkaard doing their thing back home, he had to suffer as the likes of Lex Baillie, Anton Rogan and Owen Archdeacon failed to halt the Rangers charge started by Graeme Souness.

As AC Milan were storming to victory in Europe and defeating the likes of Real Madrid 6-1 on aggregate, the Hoops were losing to the likes of Dundee and Hamilton. Sandro was not best pleased at having forked out £125 for a season book and getting no enjoyment from it. He was very vocal and spoke English in the same way that Gino D' Campo does. Nothing wrong there. It just that it can throw up some comedic moments.

On this day at Celtic Park, the Hoops were on their way to a 3-2 defeat to Dundee, having blown a 2-0 lead. All the goals were scored in the first half. My father and I would always meet Sandro on the stairway in the main stand at half-time and dissect everything.

Sandro was raging. This led to an exchange that has gone down in folklore and a phrase that my dad and myself still use if Celtic are off colour. Sandro basically screamed at the top of his voice: "That's-a-no-football-Danny-it's-a-garbage-a-gargabe-I-tell-you!" There was no punctuation just a stream of consciousness. It was brilliantly delivered and hilarious in its execution. We fell about laughing as Sandro was seething.

Fast forward to the European Cup Final of 1989 and Sandro was holding court in the club. There they were – the Dutch triumvirate leading AC Milan to glory as they demolished Steaua Bucharest 4-0. It was a devastating display as Gullit and Van Basten ran riot, grabbing a brace apiece. It was football from another dimension. Sandro turned to us at one point and said: "See Danny-that's-a-football!" We had no comeback. There was no argument.

A decade later the fates would conspire to see myself, my father and Ruud Gullit go head-to-head in Livingston! The Dutchman was appointed the manager of Newcastle United after getting...well the 'Ruud Gullit' from Chelsea. Newcastle ventured north on a tour of Scotland in July 1999 and faced Livingston at Almondvale in a pre-season friendly

I still couldn't drive at this juncture and my father regularly acted as chauffeur and drove to me various football outposts in Scotland. He stepped in again this night and as a treat I told him to sit beside me in the press box and observe. It is not often he would see his son speaking to a legend like Gullit in the after-match press conference.

He duly did.

Newcastle were tripe, despite fielding a team that included Warren Barton, Gary Speed, Kieran Dyer, and Temuri Ketsbaia. Duncan Ferguson and Alan Shearer were ruled out through injury as the Magpies lost 2-1 to the Livi Lions. The game was instantly forgettable but the assembled press pack were just desperate to get the 'nanny-goats' (quotes) from Gullit.

In Gullit strode with the familiar dread-locked style hairdo and a touch of arrogance, as if he couldn't be bothered. The Dutchman won't even remember it. As we asked him questions, Gullit became more evasive. I don't know if that is what triggered something in my dad. He started to twitch as he stood away to my right. He was edging forward all the time and I nodded as if to say 'go on then'. "Ruud, are you worried about this season coming up in the English Premiership and have you identified areas you need to strengthen bearing in mind in the past few seasons Newcastle have mounted a serious title challenge?" "God sake dad, I invite you into my office…and you dare to ask a football legend a question. What are you playing at? I thought you were just a minky pieman and part-time chauffeur?"

He wasn't, you know. If truth be told, it was a proud father/son moment and I couldn't help but laugh. The rest of the press boys were left wondering: "Who the f**k is this guy?" He just happened to be my dad. He was a real football man and probably just couldn't resist the urge to grill Gullit.

From the country that brought us Total Football, Gullit's answer to my dad's pertinent question can be summed up in two words – 'Total bollocks'. He skirted around the issue like a politician and hit out with some cliched, patronising guff that it was all about it was fitness, results didn't matter and that it was lovely to be back in Scotland.

Gullit clearly didn't know the areas to strengthen as he was sacked at St James's Park just five games into the new season.

Sandro sadly passed away a few years ago. He is still sorely missed by both of us. When I asked my dad why he asked Gullit a question that night at Livingston, he simply said: "I did it for Sandro. Ruud Gullit was one of his heroes. He would never have forgiven me if I told him that I didn't speak to him. Sandro adored Gullit and I dread to think what would have happened had we brought Sandro along." I have recurring nightmare about that scenario too!

Sandro, I was there. I can vouch for my dad. He asked your football hero a good question. It certainly wasn't a 'garbage' one and he did it all for you.

Wherever you are Sandro, I hope you are sitting with a big glass of red and the Rossoneri on a loop – "Salute!"

CHAPTER 12

A GAYLE FORCE INSIDE WEMBLEY

"I'll ask him but I'm not sure if it's gonna be his thing."
"Tony, do you want to play at Wembley tomorrow?"
"Eh?"
"We've got a spare place on the plane. We just need you to confirm, we'll change the name on the ticket and you're in."

I remember exactly where I was when that conversation took place. I was standing in the press box at Almondvale, home of Livingston FC.

Sports reporter Robert Grieve had taken a call from then Scottish Football Writers Association press team manager Kenny McDonald. Did I want to play at Wembley against the English press team? Duh! Yes, yes and yes again. I mean Wembley, it's every schoolboy's dream and it was about to come true. I just regressed and became that immature wee boy again. I kept singing to myself, "Wembley, Wembley, he's the famous Tony Haggerty and he's off to Wembley!" It sounded great in my head anyway.

The arrangements were duly made and sure enough I was about to strut my funky stuff at the home of football. Brazilian legend Pele once said this: "Wembley is the cathedral of football. It is the capital of football and it is the heart of football."

Pele never trod the hallowed sod or played at the Twin Towers but plenty of other greats had. From Puskas to Pogba, Moore to Maradona, Best to Beckham and Henry to Haggerty, all the legends had played Wembley.

There I was on a Sunday morning in June 1999, flying to London with the rest of the Scottish hacks as we prepared to face the Auld Enemy. On arrival, we were treated like football royalty. The official English team bus picked us up at the airport and we made our road trip to Wembley.

It was like FA Cup Final day in the 1970s and 1980s when the TV cameras gatecrashed the team bus and introduced viewers to the jokers and characters in the squad.

I was nearly 27 but going on 13. I just kept singing daft football songs in my head.
"Tony's going to Wembley, his knees have gone all trembly, come on you Scots…come on you Scots…!"
"Nice one Tony, nice one son, nice one Tony, let's have another one!"
"One lion on our shirt,
National pride is beaming.
Years and years of drink
Let's get 'f**ing steaming.
You're going home,
You're going home,
You're going…
England's going home.
You're going home…"
It helped pass the time.

I was a late entrant to the squad so I knew I would have to cool my jets on the bench for the first half at least. That was fine. I respected the managers decision on that one. The two teams lined up for what I'm led to believe was the last ever international match to be played at the old Wembley before it was bulldozed to make way for the current sporting theatre.

A 'who's he?' of international football had gathered on the turf. My thoughts drifted to 1977 and 1981 when I watched Scotland beat England in their ain midden. Get intae them. Let's send them homeward to think again. Defeat was not an option.

I glanced around to see if there was anybody famous in the English side. We had former Dundee and Morton stalwart Jim Duffy in our line-up. The English had former Fulham, West Ham, Blackburn Rovers and Crystal Palace defender Tony Gayle.

My moment duly arrived 10 minutes into the second half. Kenny McDonald gave me the instructions: "Go on and kick Tony Gayle, he's running the show." I was a striker to trade but everybody wanted to be up front at Wembley therefore I was flung on in a midfield role. I was wearing the No.14 jersey just as Paul Lambert did for club and country. I was no Lambert though, I was Johan Cruyff…of course I was Cruyff! A natural-born footballer was about to take the stage at Wembley wearing the No.14 jersey. I was Cruyff all day long man. One more thing, protection for ball players ref!

Right Tony Gayle you're getting it…even Cruyff did the dirty work on occasion. I sprinted on to the sacred grass at the halfway line and ran the breadth of Wembley. Wait a minute, Tony Gayle seems to be getting further away here, what's going on? I'm so unfit, I have a stitch in my stomach by now. It's warm, I feel sick.

Thud! I've clattered into Tony Gayle. I've done him…I have absolutely cemented him. I'm well proud as he goes down. I stood over him as he lay on the ground. I'm all cocky now and I give it the big 'un.
"All right Tony, my name is Tony as well, let me help you up, fella." Gayle winced in pain. He pulled himself up via my outstretched hand and said: "Cheers mate." It's as if nothing has happened. I remember thinking at the time this Tony Gayle fella is a hardy b*****d.

Scotland proceed to give the English team a skelping, easing to a 4-1 victory. Near the end it all started to get a bit out of hand. Tackles were flying in left, right and centre. I picked up the ball and noticed that the referee was checking his watch and about to blow his whistle. Crunch! "Oh my God what was that?" It felt as if my ankle had been shattered. I hit the deck. The pain was excruciating. It is the kind of tackle that when you are on the receiving end of it as a kid you start crying like a baby for your daddy.

Then I heard the voice as Tony Gayle towered over me. He sneered in his cockney accent:

"All right Tone, my name's Tony Gayle, I won the English Premier League title with Blackburn Rovers. Have some of that." Chapeau. I couldn't really complain. He picked me up this time and we both left the field hugging and laughing.

The winning Scots team were then asked to ascend the stairs to the Royal Box to collect our crystal glass trophy. Fake crowd noises were piped into the stadium as the victorious Scottish team took their bow. I was standing next to Chic Young and Jim Duffy. Then we started to taunt the English players looking up at the box: "Ray Stubbs, Lady Diana, Lord Nelson, Lord Beaverbrook, Clement Attlee, Anthony Eden, Henry Cooper, Margaret Thatcher, Tony Gayle, can you hear me? Tony Gayle can you hear me? Your boys took a hell of a beating…a hell of a beating!"

They did you know.

Our mocking was a pastiche of Norwegian commentator Bjorge Lillelien who embarked on a famous rant after his nation had defeated England 2-1 in 1981. Check it out on you tube. Key in the words 'Norwegian commentator against England 1981' and enjoy. It is a genuinely priceless piece of commentary that has gone down in history. It also very funny.

Gayle and I became the best of mates in the after-match drinks reception. I apologised profusely for deliberately going in to hurt him and he just shrugged his shoulders. He told me it was all part and parcel of the game and that he certainly wasn't going to let me away with my tackle. His medal retort was class and hilarious.

The Scottish press team completed the double over England when we beat them in Luton prior to the Euro 2000 play-off at Wembley when Don Hutchison's goal gave Craig Brown's men a memorable 1-0 victory over the Auld Enemy but we agonisingly crashed out 2-1 on aggregate to Kevin Keegan's Three Lions. I'll always have Wembley and Luton. I believe it was fellow sports journalist Lindsay Herron who coined the fabulous phrase – 'Wembley Wizards and Luton Lizards'.

You may have won the Premiership title with Blackburn Rovers, Tony Gayle. Here are two titles you do not have. You are neither a Wembley Wizard or a Luton Lizard, are you?

Have some of that.

In the nicest possible sense: 'Get that up ye Mr. Gayle!'

CHAPTER 13

A ROBIN HOOD GAME

The Football Managers office.

The inner sanctum. Sacrosanct.

It was a forbidden area for unauthorised personnel, although some bosses would dispense with that tradition and occasionally give you a personal invite. It was usually to give their version of the Gettysburg Address after a particular match.

I've lost count of the amount of stock phrases I've heard in the manager's office. "Goals change games", "the red card/the penalty kick was the turning point", "we haven't achieved anything", "we've not turned the corner", "we'll take it one game at a time", "it was a six-pointer" …blah, blah blah.

Former St Mirren boss Tom Hendrie once remarked, "We won the second half 2-1. Yeah Tom but you got pumped 3-0 in the first period!"

Danny Lennon – who miraculously guided St Mirren to League Cup glory in 2013 - gave me a fit of the giggles after a 1-0 defeat in Inverness. Danny is a fantastic guy and very funny. He is also a thoroughly decent manager.

However, on this day poor Danny got his metaphors all mixed up when he uttered: "If we had taken anything from that it would have been a Robin Hood game!"

"Eh? What are you talking about Danny?"

Yet the journalists all knew exactly what he was talking about. He meant that it would have been a form of daylight robbery had St Mirren escaped with a point. A 'Robin Hood game', the phrase still makes me chuckle thinking about it!

Most bosses just like to sound off or go 'aff their nut' from the comfort of their office. The after-match press conference is a mostly on-the-record affair and you can quote managers and players freely. The most interesting rants are usually the ones that see them go off the record, whereby the tape recorders would be switched off and they could let rip in the understanding that you would never ever print what was said.

Managers usually blasted, ranted, raged and seethed in the aftermath of a game, mostly for dramatic effect. An old journalism teacher at university used to slap me around the head repeatedly. The dearly departed Stuart Barr would often chide me: "Footballers and managers don't rant, rave, blast, seethe or rage son. What do they do? They say. Every time you quote someone - he said/she said will suffice…"
He drummed it into me.
I drummed it out of myself when it came to writing match reports for the Daily Record. I really do not know why.

Gordon Dalziel was one such manager who when he was in charge of Ayr United would allow the press boys into the sacred manager's office. Maybe it was a power play and he felt that he could control the narrative from behind his desk. Or maybe he just wanted a comfy seat. Dalziel was brand new…he was one of the good guys in the world of football management. He was a relative straight talker, took no nonsense and liked a laugh. As long as you listened.
Note to self – listen to what managers are saying after a match. It was a simple enough instruction.

Picture the scene, I am at Somerset Park as another campaign reached its climax. The players were on their summer holidays, so too were journalists and managers. It felt a bit like we were all going through the motions.

I gambled on there being lots of draws on the football coupon that weekend as everybody was past caring. I took temporary leave off my senses and stuck a £25 accumulator treble on three draws at the bookies. It was worth £2,500. As it turned out, two of the three draws had already come up. Ayr United had played out a tiresome stalemate and so had one of my other selections.

Everything now rested on Aberdeen and Kilmarnock finishing in a draw. It was 0-0 going into the closing stages. Dalziel must have had a night out to attend as he was particularly sharp to greet the press after that game. Razor sharp.

My mind was pre-occupied as the last few seconds of the Aberdeen v Killie match were being played out. We all filed into his room and Dalziel started holding court. I'm looking and seeing but I'm not hearing. I had one earpiece plugged into the portable radio and the other dangling about. I looked like Burgess Meredith, you know Rocky Balboa's trainer Micky in the famous movie franchise.

Dalziel knows I'm in the room but I'm not in the room, if you get what I mean. He starts speaking. I'm not paying attention. Then I interrupt his flow big time. You know when you let out lots of expletives because you have completely forgotten where you are? Yeah that. I lost the plot. "Ya f***ing beauty, ya f*****g dancer, get in there, c'mon, yessssss….!" At this point there must be 30 of us huddled into Dalziel's tiny room. "Tony, what the f**k is going on?"
"Sorry Gordon, I've just won the coupon Aberdeen drew 0-0 with Kilmarnock, I've won two-and-a-half grand. Sorry…you were saying?"

That was it knackered now. Dalziel launched into typical end of season fare…roll on the end of the season, but we have a duty to perform for the punters that come through the door.
"I'm sure we are all delighted for Tony getting his coupon up ya wee jammy b*****d!" And that was it. The Sunday newspaper boys weren't best pleased with me, although they did see the funny side of it all – thankfully.

We performed the necessary after-match stuff, packed up and left. I went home to East Kilbride then embarked on a night out with my pals. We decided to try a new hot spot in Glasgow called 'Tiger Tiger'. We had heard it was a good club so decided to give it a bash.

We walked in through the glass doors and we all made it past the bouncers quite easily. This was all going swimmingly well. Suddenly I felt a hand round my neck but I wasn't being frogmarched out the door. I was being frogmarched to the bar.
"Right you, get to the bar…"
I knew the voice it sounded very familiar to me but I could not place it, and the grip was so tight round my neck that I could not turn around. The voice sounded menacing enough but the guy was also laughing so at least that was a good sign. "Who was this joker?" He was a character all right or at least something beginning with 'c'.

We scrambled our way to the bar. I turned around and lo and behold it was Gordon Dalziel and his mates. We all collapsed laughing.

"That'll teach you not to f*****g listening to me after the game ya jumped-up wee p***k!"
"What'll it be Gordon?"
"Cheers Tony…step into MY office!
What do we want lads…?
This wee d**k is carrying a few…as he won the coupon the day.
Just get us a bottle of champagne.
Bolinger or Veuve Cliquot.
Whatever the dearest one is…do the honours Tony.
Have you got any bottles of champers bud for around £100?"

I thought Gordon Dalziel was joking but he most certainly wasn't.
I could not refuse him – could I?
"Dry your eyes ya wee k**b, you've got £2,400 left."
Dalziel was right. I did have £2,400 left over.
I'm glad he was listening.
Me?
I got the distinct feeling that I had just become the victim of a 'Robin Hood' game!

CHAPTER 14

THERES A CELTIC MAN AT IBROX

The first piece of writing I ever sold in my football journalism career was an interview with Rangers star Jorg Albertz. 'The Hammer', as he affectionately became known in Scotland, signed for the Light Blues in 1996 for £4million from Hamburg.

It was an apt enough nickname as the midfield powerhouse with a stunning left-foot shot often nailed it against Glasgow rivals Celtic.

Albertz hit an incredible free-kick in the New Year derby of 1997. He was 30 yards from goal and the German's lethal left foot fired the ball past Stewart Kerr before he could move at an incredible speed of 78.7mph. It was arguably the best strike of his Rangers career and certainly one of his most important as it helped the Ibrox men secure a 3-1 triumph en route to clinching Nine in a Row.

I was a student at the time with high hopes of making it as a sports reporter. I hit upon the bright idea of interviewing Albertz and Celtic star Andreas Thom. The initial premise was that Albertz was a West German while Thom started his career on the other side of the Berlin Wall. Their talents had brought both to Glasgow where they ended up on the opposite sides of another divided city. It seemed a reasonable request at the time.

I submitted my proposal to the PR machines at both clubs via a fax machine from the simulated newsroom at Glasgow Caledonian University. I didn't think for a minute that either would accept. Within an hour or so a fax from Rangers had arrived. "Tony, you've to meet John Greig at Ibrox tomorrow, 12 noon sharp." "Nice one." John Greig is going to meet me. The man voted the greatest ever Rangers player. This guy is a total legend and I'm gonna meet him. Cool. A few hours passed and then the Hoops got back in touch. "It's a knockback from Celtic, Tony – no joy."
Ach well…one out of two ain't bad.

That night this keen, wet-behind-the-ears would-be journo compiled a set of questions for 'Der Hammer'. Did he like Irn-Bru? Has he tried haggis? You know the kind of in-depth analysis that every footballer supporter laps up. My thoughts then turned to my attire. Suit, Tony, it has to be a suit, create the right impression. I had one good suit. It was bottle green! It's dark enough to pass for black, nobody will notice. You're over-thinking this, Tony. Bottle green suit it is.

I duly arrived at Ibrox the next day at 12 noon sharp. John Greig was there to meet me. He scanned my suit with his eyes. "Hello, Tony son, I'm John Greig, welcome to Ibrox, the home of the famous Glasgow Rangers! The players have just finished training, some of them should still be kicking about". Greig led me past the players' entrance and towards the dressing-room area.

Then it happened. There he was walking towards me down the narrow hall. Is that who I think it is? It is, isn't it? It's Gazza. He's walking towards Greigy and me. This Geordie drawl rang out: "Look at that green soot! Green soot man! Hey Greigy, whit ye daein' talkin' to somebody in a green soot? He looks a reet dodgy bloke!" Gazza started pointing at me as if to say, 'Who is this guy?' I couldn't resist it and said: "You don't know the half of it, Gazza!" We both burst out laughing.

Gazza proceeded to walk past us both and then, at the top of his voice, just started screaming: "There's a Celtic Man at Ibrox! There's a Celtic Man at Ibrox! There's a Celtic man at Ibrox!"

He was still screaming as he disappeared out of view. By this point, Greigy is in fits of laughter. We both headed up the famous Marble Staircase. "Jorg Albertz is in there son. He is waiting for you. He knows you are coming. If you are a Celtic supporter son, I'd keep that quiet! Enjoy your day son."

I walked into the Blue Room and sure enough, Albertz was there. He offered his hand as a welcome and we shook. "We'll start with a tour, shall we?" He proceeded to give me a guided tour of Ibrox. I enjoyed it immensely. We headed back into the Blue Room and we both took a seat before Albertz asked if I was going to try to sell the article. I explained to him that I was a journalism student and had secured a week of work experience with Total Football Magazine in England. They had expressed interest in purchasing the piece if it came up to scratch.

I conducted the interview and I did ask if he liked Irn-Bru and haggis. I could not resist it. He likes the former but is not so keen on the latter. Forgive me, I was much younger then. The German's accent was littered with 'ayes, naws' and 'nae borras'. It sounded weirdly misplaced. Yet somehow it also sounded funny to hear Albertz talk in the Glasgow vernacular. I was taken aback a bit, although he assured me that he had totally ingratiated himself into the Rangers dressing room, especially with the Scottish lads, by picking up a few choice phrases. I bet he did. We both laughed out loud at that.

Albertz confessed that he loved the Scottish accent and could make out the home-grown contingent easily enough. The only player that he couldn't really decipher was…yes, you've guessed it, Gazza! The German was in knots and said: "Nobody can understand Gazza. He speaks neither Scottish or English…it's just fluent Geordie. He is totally incoherent at the best of times. That's why we all love him. He never stops joking and clowning around. What a footballer he is though."

I then proceeded to tell Albertz the 'green soot' story. The German collapsed again with a bout of belly laughter. "That's just typical of Gazza! He's a wonderful guy and great for the morale of the dressing room. There is never a dull day with Gazza around."

The German gave me an astonishing 90 minutes of his time. He then wished me all the best with the Total Football article and for my future career. He was terrific company and diplomatic too as he didn't ask if I was a Celtic or a Rangers man.

Total Football loved my piece on Albertz and bought it off me. I stood in their offices in Bath about to negotiate with the editor. "Okay I'll play for £100, if I can get £50 for it we've won a watch," I thought. "Tony, we like this interview. Can we buy it off you for £500. Does that sound reasonable?" "Yes, thank you very much." I'm just stood there staring at the floor. My thought bubble said: "Total Football magazine just purchased my words for £500! Reasonable? It's a deal. It's a steal. It's the sale of the century. Done."

I ran outside and performed a version of Edvard Munch's 'The Scream'. £500? Is everybody at Total Football magazine mad? That was an absolute fortune for a student back then. The article still sits proudly mounted in a frame on a wall in my spare room. It means the world to me.

Whenever I look at it, I do not really think of the subject matter – Jorg Albertz. That's probably very harsh on the German who could not have been any nicer to me. Somehow the interview always reminds me of that brief encounter with Gazza. I can still hear him shouting to this day: "There's a Celtic man at Ibrox!" From Greig to Gazza to Albertz – what was there not to like?

It was a wonderful and most memorable day in my fledgling career that I have never truly forgotten. Gazza did not know me from Adam. Yet he reacted to my presence in the only way he knew how. Paul Gascoigne could and would made a joke of everything in his own irrepressible style.

I still have the 'green soot' somewhere in the back of my wardrobe. It's the 'soot', I attended my graduation from Strathclyde University in and I am loathed to part with it.

I never did let on, although Gazza was correct all along. There was indeed a Celtic man at Ibrox!

CHAPTER 15

A GOLDEN GOAL

Chances are you will never have heard of Antoine Semenyo. He is hardly a household name.

That was before October 2018, mind you.

I married my fiancée and sweetheart Caroline in a Scottish castle and it was all down to Antoine Semenyo.

Who is he then?

Semenyo just happened to be playing on loan for Newport County in October 2018 when our fates became intertwined forever. Newport County teenager Semenyo scored his first ever league goal against Stevenage and netted yours truly a whopping £11,123 on a football coupon – from a stake of just £2.

Semenyo - who was 18 at the time - was on loan from Bristol City and notched a memorable 98th-minute winner during Newport's 2-1 League Two win over Stevenage. His glorious last-gasp goal enabled Caroline and myself to book our dream wedding in a Scottish castle.

Amazingly we had scoped out the venue the day before and I fell in love with the place but the price was coming in at a five-figure sum. The spiralling costs were threatening to strangle any nuptials at birth. Our dream wedding lay in tatters…or so it seemed.

That Saturday I performed my weekly ritual of heading to my local bookies and putting on my coupons. I left the house and said to Caroline: "William Hill owes me!"

I could not have been any more prophetic if I tried.

We tied the knot at stunning Crossbasket Castle in Blantyre, Lanarkshire, on December 14, 2019. It was all thanks to Semenyo's strike. The circumstances were incredible. On the Saturday evening, I was checking my accumulator and it turned out that Newport were the only result that I was waiting for after the other five teams had delivered. It was a six-fold accumulator with both teams to score and one of them to win. I thought the match had finished 1-1. I looked at the score and it was already in the 91st minute as full-time whistles were being blown up and down the country.

Somehow the Newport County game kept going, 94… 95… 96… 97… we were in the 98th minute and suddenly there was a goal flash.

Semenyo had produced a moment of magic, drilling a low shot into the bottom corner of the Stevenage net. Cue utter bedlam. I did a lap of honour and cartwheeled around the living room. I punched the air, I kissed the coupon slip and just generally went ballistic. I totally lost it. Caroline sank to her knees in tears in total disbelief. I turned to her and screamed: "You can book that dream wedding now."

Somehow, though, that wasn't enough for me. I just had to meet Antoine Semenyo in person. My job allows me certain privileges so surely it would come through for me this time. I decided that Caroline and I should both make the 800-mile round trip to Newport's Rodney Parade stadium to thank the man who made it all happen in person.

It was the right thing to do.

Newport County could not have been any nicer. They loved the story and made all the necessary arrangements. Who wouldn't? I sorted out press accreditation as well an interview with Semenyo. Caroline and I then travelled down to attend a midweek league game against Northampton on a freezing November night in Wales.

We also decided to surprise Semenyo by presenting him with a specially engraved bottle of Jack Daniels. The message read simply: "To Antoine, a memorable goal made a dream a reality, Caroline & Tony." Antoine was very touched by his gift.

The idea was that we basically just wanted to give Antoine a souvenir that would always remind him of his first ever league goal and to tell him what it meant to us a couple. It is a moment that we will always cherish and remember.

Semenyo made more than 20 appearances for the Welsh side that season. The attacker had garnered something of a reputation since returning to parent club Bristol City, with Manchester United and Chelsea both keeping tabs on him.

Much to our regret, Semenyo could not make it north of the border to share in our big day. On the weekend of our wedding, he was too busy playing for Bristol City. We honoured the player though by naming the top table at our wedding after him.

Semenyo's goal became a massive part of our wedding story. It was the golden goal that sparked wedding bells. We had 11,123 reasons to be cheerful. Cheers Antoine…forever.

You will always be a household name to me and the wife or is it the wife and I?

CHAPTER 16

ITS NOT COMING HOME!

"It's coming home!"
Three words that are enough to give every true Scotsman the dry boak.

Cards on the table here. I can never bring myself to support England in the World Cup.

Why? I'm Scottish. End of. It's not because of some deep-rooted hatred of the English.

It's just rivalry.

So how come I ended up going head-to-head with Piers Morgan on Good Morning Britain on the morning of my 46th birthday?

Eric Dier had just stroked home the winning penalty against Colombia to set up a quarter-final against Sweden. ITV commentator Clive Tyldesley was at it again: "By the time England face Sweden in the quarter-final of the World Cup two of Uruguay, France, Belgium and Brazil will already be on the way home ... bring it on!"

It made my blood boil, so I penned a column along those lines, and I ended up on TV. I genuinely get the fact that the English always get over excited about winning the World Cup again just as they did in 1966.

If anyone had the right to savour that fervour and feeling, it was head coach Gareth Southgate. He was made the scapegoat during Euro 96 when his missed penalty against the Germans cost England a place in the final. When Southgate stepped up to the spot that night he had only taken one penalty in his career for Crystal Palace – and missed.

I quite like Southgate, he seems like a decent guy. I thought this tweet by an English fan rather wonderfully summed him up. "We salute you Gareth Southgate. You mild-mannered, waistcoat-wearing, self-deprecating, modest, articulate, calm, sensible, measured, dignified, tidy-bearded f*****g beauty."

Call it poetic justice, call it fate, but there was something beautiful about Southgate becoming the first English boss to win a World Cup penalty shootout. Only the hardest of Scottish hearts would have denied him redemption more than two decades on from his darkest England moment.

Nobody had worked harder than Southgate to unite the English team and their notorious media to work for the common goal – lifting the famous gold trophy.

What irritated me more was Southgate being asked for the umpteenth time about Euro 96. "It will never be off my back, it will live with me forever," he said. "Hopefully, this will give belief to the generations of players who follow."

That was a real touch of class and there is no easy way of saying it but Southgate has made the England team likeable again. That is no mean feat. Southgate during the 2018 World Cup looked like a man on a crusade.

By turning his own personal trauma into a life lesson, he used it as an inspiration to lead his nation to glory. If football really does come home and England do the unthinkable it would be hard not to feel some sort of happiness for Southgate but precious few others.

England duly knocked Sweden out and clinched a semi-final berth against Croatia.

It was then that I received a phone call from the GMB producers asking if wanted to go head-to-head with Morgan about why I was not supporting England.

Did I ever?

On July 11, 2018, my 46th birthday, as England got set to face Croatia in the semi-final, there I was sat in the STV studios in Glasgow, having a verbal ding-dong with Piers Morgan. I reminded him of the Auld Enemy rivalry and how the Tartan Army had waltzed off with the goalposts and parts of the Wembley pitch in 1977.It was all good-natured sporting banter.

Piers loved England. I did not. At one point he even asked me to name three Croatia players. I named the usual suspects Luka Modric, Ivan Perisic, Mario Mandzukic, Ivan Rakitic. Morgan called me a 'wee pathetic, insular Scotlander." I was extremely proud of that. I had got under his skin and really annoyed him. He then asked me to name the Croatian right back. I failed. For the record it was Sime Vrsaljko.

I left the STV studios cursing myself though as I came up with the perfect response to Morgan's Croatian right-back question the minute I stepped into the car park. For all the years that have since past I have wanted to relive the moment.

Piers Morgan: "Tony who is the Croatian right-back, I bet you can't even name him?"

Tony: "Yes I can…its 'Notcominghomesic'!!!"

"See what I did there Piers?"

To this day I dearly wish I had said that. I did have the last laugh though as England lost 2-1 to Croatia. There would be no more '1966 and all that' for the time being at least.

Memo to Piers Morgan, Clive Tyldesley, Ian Wright et al at ITV. Football was 'Notcominghomesic'…again!!!

CHAPTER 17

SLIM JIM

I never met Jim Baxter, never even saw him play. We both heard each other's voice though. I just know that in my heart of hearts I would have loved Baxter.

The Rangers legend would have fallen into the 'Davie Cooper' category as someone I greatly admired despite not favouring the team he played for.

I'd have gotten into a state of frenzy watching Baxter play for Scotland, that's for sure. I am assured that the Rangers team of the early 1960s could have held their own with most of their European counterparts.

Who knows what would have happened had Baxter not broken his leg against Rapid Vienna in 1964 and had Jock Stein not taken up the managerial role at Celtic in 1965? The course of Scottish and European football history could have been altered drastically.

Baxter helped Rangers win 10 domestic trophies from 1960 to 1965. He played against Celtic 18 times and was on the losing side just twice. The footage of Baxter toying with the English team and playing keepie-up as Scotland swept the world champions aside 3-2 at Wembley in 1967 is a wonderful watch...if you're a Scotsman that is.

It is a snapshot of his life, gallus and cocky Baxter showing the Three Lions who was boss. Sir Alex Ferguson said that Baxter's performance that day could have been set to music and that he was arguably 'the best player to play in Scottish football'.

He won the admiration of Ferenc Puskas when he turned out for the Rest of the World team against England to celebrate the centenary of the Football Association in 1963. Pele even said that Baxter could have been a Brazilian.

In 2004, Slim Jim was inducted into the Scottish Football Hall of Fame. In the December 1999 issue of World Soccer Magazine he was voted by readers into a list of the 100 greatest players of the 20th century.

BBC Scotland also ran a wonderful series called 'Only A Game' in the 1980s. It was a warts-and-all look at Scottish football from every perspective. In the episode entitled: 'The Player', Baxter featured prominently.

Former Leeds and Scotland skipper Billy Bremner recalled the time Baxter faced Italy in a World Cup qualifier at Hampden in 1965. The finals, of course, would be held in England but Baxter only played in two qualifiers due to injury problems.

Bremner takes up the story: "The two team line-ups were pinned up on the wall. Baxter was scanning the names to see who his direct opponent was: Rivera? I'll Rivera him when we get out there!" Gianni Rivera was Italian football's golden boy. He won three Serie As and two European Cups with AC Milan and earned 60 caps for his country, scoring 14 goals but reputations meant nothing to Baxter. Bremner continued: "Jim told me just to give him the ball all the time. When the game started, I kept giving the ball to Jim. Every now and then I heard him shout: 'That's wan, that's two, that's three…' Jim had counted to 10 and I sidled up to him and I asked: 'Jim what's with all the counting?' He just looked at me and said: 'I've stuck the ball through Rivera's legs 10 times and counting. Hey, Rivera, they told me you could play!'
It is a brilliant tale which totally sums Baxter up. Scotland won the game 1-0.
If you watch John Greig's winning goal on YouTube, you will notice it is Baxter who takes the ball from the goalkeeper and then plays the most exquisite slide rule pass into the path of his Rangers team-mate who slams it into the net. The pass is weighted to perfection. It is executed with cold, calculated precision. Utterly sublime.

Baxter had no equal. The modern-day equivalent and immediate comparison would be Paul Gascoigne. Sadly he also had well-versed off-the-field problems. Tragically Baxter died from cancer of the pancreas in 2001.

I feel privileged and honoured that I spoke to him though and here's how.

Baxter liked a drink. He also liked a bet. He used to hold court in the bar and liked to bet the locals for both cash and bevvy. Now Baxter had a habit of phoning the Daily Record Sports desk with all sorts of trivia questions which he believed we would know the answers to. He was very friendly with our Sports Editor at the time, Jim Traynor, and it had become a regular occurrence to field Jim's 'Question of Sport'.

One day Baxter duly phoned Traynor's landline.
"Whit, aww Jim you're joking…nobody is going to know that."
"Know what?"
Traynor sighed and reeled off a question that had four parts to it. The subject matter was darts.
"Who won the Embassy World Professional Darts Championship in 1983?
Where did he win it?
What was the final checkout he won it on?
What was unique about the win?"
Traynor's shoulders slumped and he said: "Anybody know this?"
I moved forward. "Yeah, I know it Jim."
"He wants all the answers Tony, there must be cash and drink riding on it."
"I know all the answers Jim…tell him this…"
Before I could say another word, Traynor has thrust the telephone into my hand.
"Hello, who am I speaking to?"
Baxter hailed from Hill O'Beath in Fife. His intonation had a slight lilt.
"It's Tony Haggerty, Jim, how are you fella?"
"I'm great Tony son, now there is a lot at stake here, do you know the answers? If you do can you speak loud and clear down the phone, son?"

"I do Jim…the answers in order: Keith Deller, The Jollees in Stoke, 138 checkout and Deller became the first qualifier in history to win the World Professional Darts Championship."
Baxter let out a joyous shriek followed by the words "A telt ye, A telt ye all, you all owe me, pay up, pay up! Tony son, you have just won Jim Baxter a fortune in cash and a wee drink as well. You're a legend Tony!"

Baxter rarely misplaced a pass in the whole of his career but he had badly misplaced his words in this instance. There were two people standing holding a phone. One of us was a bona-fide Scottish football legend. I will give you all a clue – it certainly wasn't me!

Baxter remains a Scottish football icon. Whenever I think of Slim Jim, I can still hear his high-pitched scream of delight. It makes me smile to this day knowing that Baxter had stumped his audience and won his bet and by some quirk of fate I had helped him achieve that. I was claiming an assist.

For once Baxter was not in the soup.

Please don't ask me how I knew the answers to Baxter's darts trivia questions when football is supposed to be my game.

I just did.

If anybody out there wants to put my darts trivia knowledge to the test once more then be my guest…'Game On!'

CHAPTER 18

THE 'INVINCIBLES'

The heavens opened and the lightning bolt struck. Hampden Park and time seemed to stand still for a split second. Scottish football history was about to be made in the 2017 Scottish Cup Final as Celtic faced Aberdeen.

The Hoops, under new boss Brendan Rodgers, were on the brink of the domestic Treble. The match was evenly poised at 1-1 two minutes into stoppage time.

That's when the 'Wizard of Oz' – Celtic midfielder Tom Rogic – decided to take matters into his own hands...or was it twinkle-toed feet? The Australian suddenly picked up the ball on the halfway line and slalomed his way through the Dons defence before squeezing a shot past Aberdeen goalkeeper Joe Lewis. 2-1 to Celtic.

Cue utter bedlam in the stands as well as lightning in the sky. Rogic's strike was no ordinary goal. It would forever become known as the 'Invincible' strike. It was the most fitting climax to an incredible season.

Celtic became the first team in Scottish football history to win the domestic Treble without losing a single game. Rodgers' team played 47 games in all competitions. They won 43 and drew four and lost NONE.

Rogic's effort was a goal like no other. In a season like no other. It all seemed so apt for Celtic when you consider the Hoops marketed themselves as 'a club like no other'.

On that fateful and historic day at Hampden, the Hoops had attempted to do something no other Scottish football club had achieved. To go a whole campaign undefeated. With the notable exceptions of Tommy Gemmell's and Stevie Chalmers strikes in the 1967 European Cup Final, no Celtic goal has ever been celebrated with as much gusto than Rogic's 'Invincible' strike.

I should know. I was there alongside my dad and my nephew Matthew. The unconfined joy etched on every Celtic supporter's face during the wild goal celebrations told their own story.

As a sports journalist I am usually very reserved on such occasions, even when watching my team, because of the nature of my profession. In the sodding rain at Hampden, I just thought 'sod it'. All thoughts of neutrality went out the window and I just lost it. Think 'Tasmanian devil meets Yosemite Sam' and you would still not even be remotely close as to how mental my reaction was to Rogic's goal.

It felt wonderful to act like a proper football fan for the first time in nearly two decades of writing about the 'beautiful game' from the relative sanity of the press box. It is a treasured football moment that will live with me forever.

Despite the happiness, I also remember being struck by an overwhelming wave of sadness and a bout of emptiness. I was totally ecstatic...yes. I was there with my dad and nephew and it was magic to share the experience with them both. It was a wonderful achievement and one that will never be done again. Yet I felt as though there was something missing. There most certainly was. It was my brother Danny. We had grown up watching Celtic together with my dad since we were kids. We had dreamed of days like this. We had been through so many football experiences together growing up. Whenever I shut my eyes and think of my happy place, it inevitably involves football, my dad, my brother and Celtic. The next generation of the family (Matthew) was already following in our footsteps.

Work commitments had prevented my brother from being at Hampden on that historic day. It pains me that I did not share it with my brother and best pal. Danny would have loved this moment. I should have bought him a ticket and somehow demanded that he travelled up from down south to be there with us. It remains a regret to this day.

My brother has a saying: 'Life's great, innit?'. Life did feel great when Rogic pulled the trigger and scored that goal. One assumes that only Lisbon in 1967 can compare to the emotion and euphoria felt by every Celtic supporter of my generation that day. I am 47 years young.

In season 2016/17, Celtic set a new Premiership record points total of 106. The Hoops scored an incredible 106 goals, another record. They also set a new landmark for the most league wins in a campaign, coming out on top in 34 of their 38 matches. Celtic even eclipsed the Lisbon Lions' 50-year record after going 27 matches unbeaten from the start of the season. The Lions' run was halted at 26.

Rogic's goal stands out like a green and white beacon in the club's illustrious recent history. For every Celtic supporter, the 'Invincible' strike is certainly up there. It falls just short of being comparable with the two goals scored by Jock Stein's side in the Estadio Nacional Stadium in Lisbon on the May 25, 1967.

Although with one swish of his right boot the Australian had made sure that he etched his name into Scottish football and Celtic folklore. Rogic had also carved an indelible mark in the hearts and minds of every member of the Celtic family.

Just like the Lisbon Lions before them, Rodgers' 'Invincibles' squad of 2016/17 ensured that that they will similarly be revered. The current Celtic manager Neil Lennon once famously spoke of bringing back the 'Thunder' during his first stint at the Hoops helm. Under Rodgers, it was Rogic who brought forth the 'Lightning'.

My brother turned 50 this year. I thought nothing could ever make up for the fact that Danny missed Celtic's 'Invincible' match and Rogic's goal. Danny should have been at Hampden, standing shoulder to shoulder with his dad, his brother and his nephew, cheering on his boyhood idols.

I got married in December 2019. My brother was my best man. What do you get a guy who is happy and content with his lot in life? It finally came to me in a blinding flash.

I got my redemption shot for not forcing the issue and getting my brother a ticket for that cup final. On the morning of my wedding, I took Danny for a run in my car. We drove to Parkhead and walked up the Celtic Way, past the wonderful statue of big Billy McNeill (Cesar) proudly holding aloft the European Cup.

Third batch. Row four. Eleven in from the right. We both looked down. In grey slate was the Celtic shamrock crest. Inscribed were the words: "To Big Dan, Life's Great, Innit!"

It was my wedding gift to him. Tears and snotters followed. It may be twisted 'Rogic' and whilst my brother is not an 'Invincible' at least his stone on the Celtic Way makes him an immortal.

I can live with that.

CHAPTER 19

A BA' HAIR!

John Lambie was a unique man. He was a cigar-smoking, doo-fancying, whisky-swilling legend. He also liked to swear - a lot.

The PC brigade would have hated him. The Scottish football press corps loved him. He was brilliant and I thought the world of him.

The anecdote that follows is classic Lambie. It was also the day the former Partick Thistle, Hamilton and Falkirk manager gave me a footballing education – 'Lambie style'.

Partick Thistle had drawn a league game at Firhill and the great man was one of the few managers who always addressed the press from the safety of his office. He loved to hold court after every match.

There was no need for press officers in Lambie's day. He would have chased them anyway. He was a fantastic raconteur. He lived for the verbal combat with journalists and so-called 'experts' of the game.

He would sit in the big swivel chair, puffing on a cigar and necking a dram, waiting for the questions from the assembled hacks.
On this occasion, Lambie was in full rant mode. His face was scarlet. He just happened to look up, caught my gaze and was staring directly at me.

"Hey, you, do you know how f***ing close we came to winning that f***ing game, son? I'll f***ing tell you how close we f***ing came. A ba' hair son ... a f***ing ba' hair! For the so-called journalists among you that is spelt 'b, f***ing a, apostrophe f***ing hair!'"

By this point my shoulders have collapsed and I am doubled over with laughter. Every day is indeed a school day because I certainly wasn't aware that a 'ba' hair' was an actual unit of football measurement.

I did what every self-respecting sports journalist does when presented with quotes that are often described as 'manna from heaven'. I reproduced the exchange verbatim in my Daily Record match report for Monday's newspaper. I reported for duty on the Monday morning, sat at my desk and waited patiently. Lo and behold, my landline rang at roughly 10.01. It was Lambie…I knew it would be. He was screaming down the line at me.

"Hey, you, ya haufwit, what are you f***ing doin' to me? Why did you f***ing print that, word for f***ing word. Am I the only b******ing f***ing manager in Scottish f***ing football that f***ing swears?"

As quick as a flash I replied: "No John but nobody swears quite like you. "It's an art form. Read the paragraph. It's Shakespeare – John Lambie style!"

To which Lambie replied: "F***ing Shakspearean? Aye, I guess you could be f***ing right son. "I phoned to give you a f***ing bollocking son. You've actually just made my f***ing day. You were barred from Firhill but I'll f***ing see you next week. I look f***ing forward to it!"

That was Lambie in a nutshell. He was maniacal and comical, one of Scottish football's greatest characters. Above all else, Lambie was a football man. He was a fantastic man-manager and a great motivator.

He defined the term old-school.

I will always be eternally grateful that our paths crossed in my early days. Not only was it an education but also a total privilege. I admit to shedding a tear when I heard that Lambie had passed away.

The memories of our encounters will live with me for eternity.

Rest In F***ing Peace John.

CHAPTER 20

HERO WORSHIP

People often ask me, what is the best piece I have written or the most memorable interview I have conducted for the Daily Record.

My answer is always the same. I do not have one. Although I do have a favourite moment. It has been a fantastic two decades serving the best newspaper in the country, giving me some wonderful moments which I have endeavoured to share with you.

The Henrik Larsson pull-out helped me meet the great man and I presented Diego Maradona, the finest player to ever grace this planet, with a trophy at Celtic Park. I also asked Brazilian footballing legend Pele a question when he made a public appearance in Glasgow.

One highlight shines out like a beacon though. It was the night I introduced my father, Danny, to European Cup winner Bobby Murdoch. I was asked to appear on a panel with three of Jock Stein's legendary Lisbon Lions in the Brazen Head pub.

It was a Q&A with anecdotes thrown in for good measure. Jimmy 'Jinky' Johnstone, Bertie Auld, Bobby Murdoch and yours truly? We have amassed an astonishing three European Cup winners' medals between us!

On the drive down to the Glasgow hostelry, my dad casually turned to me and said: "Did you know that Bobby Murdoch is my all-time football hero, son?" "Er... no I didn't. Why didn't I know this, dad?"

We walked into the boozer and sure enough the three Lisbon Lions were already there. By way of a quick introduction, I turned to my dad and said, "Dad, this is Jimmy Johnstone... this is Bertie Auld... and this is Bobby Murdoch. Bobby this is my dad Danny." My old man dryly quipped: "I know who they are son!" Bobby then turned to my dad and said: "Hi Danny, do you fancy a pint?"

The two men then started to chew the fat before disappearing to the bar. Bobby then placed his hand on my father's shoulder as if he were embracing a long-lost pal. He was that kind of guy. Bobby Murdoch was an absolute gem of a fella who is sorely missed.

It was the most beautiful football-related sight I have ever seen. I had a lump in my throat and had to dive away to enjoy a private moment. I am not ashamed to admit that I wept uncontrollably.

Words are my currency, and I was totally lost for them. Here was my dad sitting there with his hero and chatting to three members of the greatest ever Celtic team and the greatest ever Scottish club side. He was sat there conversing to three Lisbon Lions as if it was the most natural thing in the world.

And it occurred to me that history had come full circle. My father had taken me to see my own football hero King Kenny Dalglish back in 1976/77. Here I was repaying that favour and introducing him to his all-time favourite player and football idol. How could you ever top that?

It has been an absolute pleasure and a privilege to serve as a reporter for the Daily Record. In football parlance, the Daily Record was the only newspaper I ever wanted to write for. It helped open doors to the good and the great…and sometimes the not so good and oft-times the downright rotten.

That is why nothing ever came close to seeing my dad in the company of three Lisbon Lions and hugging Bobby Murdoch. The highlight of my career? It is the greatest achievement of my two decades spent as a sports journalist bar none. It always will be. Funnily enough my dad remains my hero to this very day. He still will be long after he is gone. Thank you, father, for introducing me to the beautiful game.

CHEERS TO YOU ALL FOR READING.

ABOUT THE AUTHOR

Tony gained a joint honours degree and postgraduate diploma from Strathclyde University before joining the Daily Record in 1999.

He spent over 20 years covering football, darts, boxing and American football.

Tony has appeared on national radio and TV and was once a regular contributor on STV programme 'Scotsport First'.

He left the newspaper industry in October 2019 in order to go back to Glasgow University to undertake a PGDE in teaching English (Secondary).

Tony is married to Caroline, they have no kids, but they have two dogs, a Golden Retriever named Oscar and a Romanian rescue Chihuahua/terrier cross called Evie.

This is Tony's first attempt at writing and publishing a book.

Printed in Great Britain
by Amazon

19844104R00058